A QUESTION OF SPORT

COMPILED BY
MIKE ADLEY
JOHN TAIT
and
RAY STUBBS

BBC BOOKS

Picture Credits *Action Photos* (R. Francis) Sheene, page 97; *All-Sport* all photos pages 10 and 18, Moon, Hoddle, Schoenlebe, page 26, all photos pages 34, 42, 50, Khan, page 54, all photos pages 58, 66 and 74, Davies, page 81, all photos page 82, Reid, page 89, all photos page 90, Miller, page 94, Dalglish, Beamon, Brabham, page 98, Cooman, page 105, Gullit, Ashford, Spitz, page 106, Gower, Barnes, Decker-Slaney, page 114, all photos page 122; *Associated Press* Lineker, page 38, Butcher, page 57; *Associated Sports Photography* Lynch, page 57; *Mike Brett* Deans, page 98, Dooley, page 106, Hanley, page 114; *Colorsport* Cram, page 46; *David Muscroft* Stevens, page 26; *Henry Ormesher* Lawrenson, page 65; *Mike Patrick* Nielsen, page 73; *Radio Times* front cover and page 7; *Sportsfile* Molby, page 81; *Universal Pictorial Press* Jeffrey, page 105, Payton, page 121; *West Ham Photos* Cottee, page 105. All remaining photos are BBC copyright.

Published by BBC Books
A division of BBC Enterprises Limited
Woodlands, 80 Wood Lane, London W12 0TT

First published 1988

© BBC Enterprises Limited 1988

ISBN 0563 20647 0

Typeset in 10/11 Times by Ace Filmsetting Ltd,
Frome, Somerset and printed in England by
Redwood Burn Ltd, Trowbridge, Wiltshire.

CONTENTS

5 · **Foreword**

6 · A Word from the Captains

8 · **Game 1**
Nigel Mansell, Bryan Robson, Linford Christie, John Rutherford

16 · **Game 2**
Judy Simpson, Lloyd Honeyghan, Eric Bristow, Peter Beardsley

24 · **Game 3**
Colin Deans, Roger Black, Ian Rush, Steve Davis

32 · **Game 4**
Hana Mandlikova, Charlie Nicholas, Sam Torrance,
Peter Scudamore

40 · **Game 5**
Virginia Leng, David O'Leary, Mike Harrison, Terry Marsh

48 · **Game 6**
Trevor Steven, Mike Gatting, Peter Fleming, Lucinda Green

56 · **Game 7**
Terry Butcher, Frank Bruno, Liz Lynch, Rob Andrew

64 · **Game 8**
Jack Buckner, Cliff Thorburn, Herol Graham, Mark Lawrenson

72 · **Game 9**
Mo Johnston, Chris Broad, Walter Swinburn, Hans Nielsen

80 · **Game 10**
Jan Molby, Nick Faldo, Jimmy White, Jonathan Davies

88 · **Game 11**
Peter Reid, Todd Bennett, Martin Bell, Ian Botham

96 · **Game 12**
Barry Sheene, George Best, Steve Smith, Lynn Davies

104 · **Game 13**
Tony Cottee, Adrian Moorhouse, Nelli Cooman, John Jeffrey

112 · **Game 14**
Mark Elia, Clive Allen, Allan Lamb, Kirsty Wade

120 · **Game 15**
Walter Payton, Howard Clark, Helena Sukova, Daley Thompson

FOREWORD

On Monday 5 January 1970 *A Question of Sport* was first transmitted on BBC Television. Looking back at the *Radio Times* for that week, those programmes in colour were still bracketed in italics, so *A Question of Sport* and *Z Cars*, which followed it, lacked the lustre of television's latest innovation.

It was down to the then Question Master, David Vine, and Captains Henry Cooper and Cliff Morgan to add their own brand of colour with their guests in that very first programme: Britain's 1968 Olympic silver medallist Lillian Board, international football legends George Best and Tom Finney, and cricket's Ray Illingworth, who later became the first England Captain since Douglas 'Bodyline' Jardine to regain the Ashes in Australia. The proof of its success is that 18 years and 213 shows later the programme has prime place in BBC-1 schedules at 8.30 pm on Thursdays.

Today, those fashionable sweaters of Messrs Coleman, Beaumont and Hughes are in living colour, and the parade of the world's top sporting stars have kept the programme consistent alongside *EastEnders*, *Dallas* and *Dynasty* in the weekly top ten.

In this book, written by the Manchester-based production team of the programme, you have an opportunity to be David, Emlyn, Bill or any of their famous guests, and answer the questions which all reflect the rounds of the televised show. It's a chance to recreate the fun, entertainment and challenge of *A Question of Sport* in your own home.

Mike Adley,
Producer, *A Question of Sport* BBC Manchester

A WORD FROM THE CAPTAINS

'The last time I saw that face, it had a hook in it'.

Insults are fair game in the heat of a rugby scrum. There, you can at least answer back, but during *A Question of Sport*, where the remark has reduced your team mates and audience to hysterics—what do you do? To Les Dawson, thank you.

Fifty or so programmes facing Emlyn and David have left me many memorable moments, and we are good friends both on and off the television, but that doesn't mean I'm prepared to let Emlyn and his team win to keep the series even. Winning is as important to me now as it was on the rugby field.

Today, as Captain, my role is one of encouragement and tactics. Encouragement on Thursday evenings when many of the guests would prefer to do 15 rounds with Frank Bruno than appear—until the closing music fades, that is, when they always ask to come back again. My advice on tactics is: don't rush in, wait a few moments, and always look at the feet for the visual questions. That's how Jim Watt became Anne Hobbs. Bryan Robson became Gillian Gilks and Sue Barker became Alan Minter!

Good Luck

Getting hit with a handbag is one thing, getting a whack from a royal handbag is another . . . . Many of you will have seen me nearly get clobbered by the Princess Royal – mind you, I had mistaken her for the flat-racing jockey John Reid so a 'Royal Rap' was better than the Tower of London. I must say though that when Princess Anne appeared on the 200th edition of *A Question of Sport* it was the highlight of my time on the programme.

   Sitting opposite Billy Beaumont has been a real education; I was going to say it's easier than facing him in a rugby scrum, but having heard him answer some of the questions we've been asked I'm not so sure. Me, I've always enjoyed quizzes. We used to ask each other sports questions on the Liverpool coach. I didn't get many right then either. The important thing on *A Question of Sport* is the atmosphere – it's the same every week, we always have a laugh, we play to win, but we smile when we lose.

   Hope you enjoy the quiz . . . it's good stuff. See you, pal!

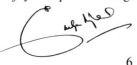

6

BILL BEAUMONT

Bill played his first game for Fylde Rugby Club in 1971 as a full back. After one full season in their premier side he was chosen to play for his county, Lancashire. He was capped for England under-23s against Tonga in 1974, coming on as a substitute, and a year later gained his first full cap against Ireland in Dublin, on the losing side. He toured Australia with England that year and went on to make 33 successive appearances for England – a record – captaining the side on 22 occasions from 1978 to 1982. In 1980 he had the distinction of leading his country to the Triple Crown and Grand Slam. He toured with the British Lions twice, visiting New Zealand in 1977 and South Africa in 1980, and playing 19 matches in all. On the last occasion he captained the side, the first Englishman to do so for 47 years.

Bill's rugby career ended prematurely in 1982 when he was forced to leave the Moseley pitch after a bang on his head during a county match, and was later advised to retire from the game on medical grounds. Shortly before this he had taken over the captaincy of *A Question of Sport* from Gareth Edwards, and has amply demonstrated his tactical flair and leadership skills on countless occasions since in his weekly duel of wits with Emlyn.

EMLYN HUGHES

Emlyn had plenty of experience of captaincy before he joined *A Question of Sport*. He skippered club and country during a marvellous career in professional football that spanned 19 years. Born in Barrow, the son of a rugby league player, it was Blackpool who first recognised his potential but Liverpool who took advantage of his enthusiasm and determination to win.

'Crazy Horse', as he became known to the Liverpool fans, arrived at Anfield in March 1967. For the next 12 years he was a regular in the side and helped the club win the League title three times and made three FA Cup Final appearances during this time—he picked up a winners medal after the 1974 final against Newcastle. In Europe the UEFA Cup came to Anfield twice, and it was Emlyn who collected the Champions Cup after a famous Liverpool win in Rome in 1977.

Emlyn also established himself as one of the mainstays of the England side. His first cap was against Wales in 1970, and he made 62 appearances in all, leading England out on 22 occasions. One thing still rankled with him—he'd failed to win the League Cup, but when the great Liverpool side of the early 1970s broke up he moved to Wolves and led them to their 1980 League Cup Final victory against Nottingham Forest, the team that had prevented him from completing a set of domestic trophy successes with Liverpool. His playing career ended with spells at Hull, Swansea, Mansfield and Rotherham where he was player-manager for 18 months.

GAME 1

This week's guests come from the worlds of motor racing, athletics, soccer and rugby union. Bill is joined by Nigel Mansell and Linford Christie, whilst Emlyn has persuaded Bryan Robson to join him, along with John Rutherford.

✕ BILL'S TEAM ✕

NIGEL MANSELL Fought off serious injury to become one of the world's top Formula One drivers. Who'll ever forget how he survived a burst tyre in Australia at 200 mph and lost the world title by two points? A keen golfer renowned for banging his head on the desk after getting an answer wrong in front of Princess Anne when she appeared on the show.

LINFORD CHRISTIE Britain's number one sprinter, who took the best in Europe apart over 100 m in 1986. He's as good indoors as out—but that's over 200 m. Reliably expected to help Bill out with the athletics questions in the show, and has a great sense of humour. On one occasion had to be told to quieten down after Bill told him a joke. Bill hasn't told anyone else what the joke was!

✕ EMLYN'S TEAM ✕

BRYAN ROBSON As a schoolboy he was told he was too small to make a professional footballer, yet he went on to captain England in two World Cups, and led Manchester United to FA Cup Final victory! Highly respected around the world as a midfield player—but, like Nigel, has a habit of diving in too soon and getting the answers wrong on *A Question of Sport.* Emlyn's not much help in that direction either!

JOHN RUTHERFORD Scotland's most capped fly-half who was with the Scottish side that won the Triple Crown and the Grand Slam in 1984 and appeared in the first World Cup 'down under' in the summer of '87. Bill ducks his home questions on rugby with alarming frequency—will John do the same or listen to Emlyn's advice?

Pictureboard

1

2

3

4

Home & Away

NIGEL
Nikki Lauda took the 1984 world championship with five Grand Prix wins—but who, with seven wins, was runner-up?

In which country is 'Camogie' the premier sport for women?

BRYAN
Which Canadian soccer club did Peter Beardsley play for?

Four Britons challenged Ali for the world heavyweight title: Henry Cooper, Brian London and Joe Bugner were three. Who was the fourth?

LINFORD
Where were the first official World Indoor Athletics Championships held in 1987?

Which sport uses an Albion, a New National and a Long Western?

JOHN
Which country did New Zealand defeat in the final to become the first winners of rugby union's World Cup?

If 20 equals 3 and 19 equals 1, what does 18 equal?

BILL
In which competition do the winners collect the Russell Cargill Trophy?

The 100 Guineas Cup began as a race around the Isle of Wight. What major international event is it now?

EMLYN
In 1895 the fitters and joiners of the Furness Withy shipyard played for the Viscountess of Furness Cup. By what name is that trophy now known?

From where to where would you measure a boxer's reach?

One-Minute Round

☆ BILL'S TEAM ☆

1 (1 pt) Rugby: in which year did the international championship end in a five-way tie?

2 (1 pt) Motor racing: whose record of 27 Grand Prix wins did Alain Prost beat in 1987?

3 (1 pt) Athletics: at which Olympic Games did Alan Wells win the 100 metres gold?

4 (1 pt) Tennis: who was the 1987 men's singles champion at Wimbledon?

5 (2 pts) Soccer: which two sides played in the 1987 FA Cup Final?

6 (2 pts) At which famous sporting venues would you find the following:
a) Swinley Bottom
b) Stable Junction
c) Sunset Bend

1 (1 pt)   Soccer: what was the last League side managed by Sir Alf Ramsey?

2 (1 pt)   Eventing: who won her first Badminton title on Be Fair in 1973?

3 (1 pt)   Rugby: which country, led by Graham Mourie, beat all four home countries on the 1978 tour of the British Isles?

4 (1 pt)   Racing: on which horse did Geoff Lewis win his only Derby in 1971?

5 (2 pts)   Tennis: which British pair were the 1987 Wimbledon mixed doubles champions?

6 (2 pts)   Where would you find the following:
a) Capability's Cutting
b) Woe-Be-Tide
c) Clearways

GAME 1
Mystery Personality

14

GAME 1
ANSWERS

PICTUREBOARD

1 Alain Prost, French World Formula 1 motor racing champion in both 1985 and 1986. Winner of more Grand Prix races than any other driver, beating Jackie Stewart's total of 27.
2 Carl Lewis, the American athlete who was four times gold medallist in the 1984 Olympics at 100 m, 200 m, the 4 × 100 m relay and the long jump.
3 Viv Anderson/Clive Allen. Manchester United defender Viv Anderson challenges Spurs player Clive Allen. Both are England internationals.
4 Terry Holmes, scrum-half for Cardiff, Wales and the British Lions. Now moved to rugby league with Bradford Northern, but forced to retire through injury.

HOME & AWAY

NIGEL (HOME)
Alain Prost. Lauda won the title by a mere half-point. Prost's seven wins equalled Jim Clark's record for a season set in the 60s.

(AWAY)
Ireland. Started around 1900 in Dublin—it's a 12-a-side stick-and-ball game for women that's a form of hurling played in two halves of 25 minutes each.

BRYAN (HOME)
Vancouver Whitecaps. Played for them in two spells: the first in 1982, the second after Manchester United didn't sign him after a loan period.

(AWAY)
Richard Dunn. Cooper and London challenged in the 60s, Bugner and Dunn in the 70s. All failed to win.

LINFORD (HOME)
Indianapolis. They are recognised as the first official World Indoor Championships. France staged the World Indoor Games in 1985.

(AWAY)
Archery. They are differing rounds in distance and levels of competition for toxophilites.

JOHN (HOME)
France. The All Blacks were awesome throughout the tournament, winning the final 29–9.

(AWAY)
7. They are all opposite numbers on a dartboard.

BILL (HOME)
Middlesex Sevens.

(AWAY)
The America's Cup. In 1851 the New York Yacht Club raced by invitation against 17 British boats, and won. Six years later they put up the trophy as a perpetual challenge.

EMLYN (HOME)
The Littlewoods Cup. Formerly the Milk Cup and League Cup. The trophy was found in an antique shop and resurrected.

(AWAY)
From fingertip to fingertip, with both arms outstretched from the sides of the body.

ONE-MINUTE ROUND

BILL'S TEAM
1 1973.
2 Jackie Stewart.
3 The 1980 Moscow Games.
4 Pat Cash (Australia).
5 Spurs and Coventry (Coventry won 3–2).
6 a) Ascot   b) The Cresta Run   c) Kyalami Grand Prix race circuit.

EMLYN'S TEAM
1 Birmingham City.
2 Lucinda Green (née Prior-Palmer).
3 New Zealand (the All Blacks).
4 Mill Reef.
5 Jeremy Bates and Jo Durie.
6 a) Burghley (3-day eventing)   b) Turnberry (golf)   c) Brands Hatch (motor-racing).

MYSTERY PERSONALITY

BILL'S TEAM   Pat Cash, the 1987 Wimbledon men's singles champion and member of the Australian Davis Cup winning team.
EMLYN'S TEAM   Malcolm Marshall, the West Indian pace bowler who plays cricket for Hampshire.

GAME 2

A tricky mixture this week, with darts, boxing, athletics and soccer providing the guests. Heptathlete Judy Simpson and darts' Eric Bristow join Emlyn, with Bill hoping that Lloyd Honeyghan will pull no punches, and Peter Beardsley will score the 'goals'.

☆ BILL'S TEAM ☆

LLOYD HONEYGHAN Shocked the boxing world in 1986 by taking the world welterweight crowns off Don 'Cobra' Curry. A snappy dresser who always looks as much the part out of the ring as in it. Late on to the set for his last appearance on the show—deciding which sweater to wear—and no-one was prepared to tell him to hurry it up! Well, would you?

PETER BEARDSLEY Few players could persuade Liverpool to shell out a record £1.8 million for their services—but he did! Established himself with England in the World Cup in Mexico in 1986, and hasn't looked back since. Lining up alongside Bill and Lloyd Honeyghan, his captain for the show has already been taking bets that he's as quick in the 1-minute round as he is on the pitch.

☆ EMLYN'S TEAM ☆

JUDY SIMPSON It's ladies first, and Judy leads off each round in this show. And why not? Already she has a Commonwealth Games gold medal to her credit, as well as a European bronze, and with Olympic experience already behind her she is likely to stay one of Britain's top lady athletes throughout the '80s. Worries about Emlyn's indecisiveness, and her own spelling.

ERIC BRISTOW This lad's spell as the world's number one darts player had the rest of them suffering the 'seven year itch'—that's how long it lasted. Over 30 major darts titles, with his first world championship won back in 1980. 'The Crafty Cockney' really didn't attempt to bribe the producer for the questions in advance—and anyway, his love of cricket and football is a strong enough back-up.

GAME 2
Pictureboard

1

2

3

4

?

18

Home & Away

JUDY
Ramona Neubert broke the world heptathlon record twice in 1981, and became the first European champion in 1982. Which country did she represent?

LLOYD
Which British boxer twice challenged Milton McCrory for the WBC world welterweight title?

ERIC
Who is the darts player with most appearances for his country in internationals?

PETER
Nottingham Forest won the European Cup in 1979 and 1980. Name one of the sides they beat in the final.

EMLYN
On 8 February 1985, Sheffield United's match against Oldham was postponed—for what unusual reason?

BILL
Who captained Scotland to the Triple Crown and Grand Slam in 1984?

What would you be watching if you saw a 'chain crew' called on to the field?

The 1877 Boat Race provided an incident unique in the race's history—what was it?

In Turkey it's Yagli, in Russia it's Sambo. Cumberland and Cornish are variations here at home—but what's the sport?

With which sport would you connect the 'Bagshot Scramble' and the 'Circuit of the Duckpond'?

In which sport did the Essex cricketer David Acfield win a Commonwealth Games team gold medal?

Tennis. Complete the sequence: John McEnroe, Tom Okker, Pat Dupre, Brian Gottfried, Rod Frawley, Tim Mayotte, Chris Lewis, Pat Cash and Boris Becker. Who was next?

One-Minute Round

1 (1 pt) Phil Neale played soccer for Lincoln City. Which county cricket side did he captain in 1987?

●

2 (1 pt) Darts: who scored the first televised nine-dart finish at 501?

●

3 (1 pt) Athletics: a javelin champion, she broke the British record for the heptathlon in 1981. Who was she?

●

4 (1 pt) Cycling: name the American who won the 1986 Tour de France.

●

5 (2 pts) Racing: name the two jockeys who rode Red Rum to his three Grand National wins.

●

6 (3 pts) Their names sound like forms of transport—complete them.
a) Soccer: Ray (?)
b) Cricket: Bill (?)
c) Soccer: Franz (?)

●

1 (1 pt) Rugby: who, in November 1986, became the most-capped prop forward in the world?

●

2 (1 pt) Boxing: at what weight was John H. Stracey a world champion?

●

3 (1 pt) Soccer: who were the last British club to win the UEFA Cup?

●

4 (1 pt) Athletics: how many individual world records—indoor and out—did Seb Coe break?

●

5 (2 pts) Motor racing: since the war only three tracks have staged the British Grand Prix. Brands Hatch was one, but name the other two.

●

6 (3 pts) Their names sound like forms of creases—who are they?
   a) Racing: Phil (?)
   b) Soccer: David (?)
   c) Snooker: Neal (?)

●

GAME 2
Mystery Personality

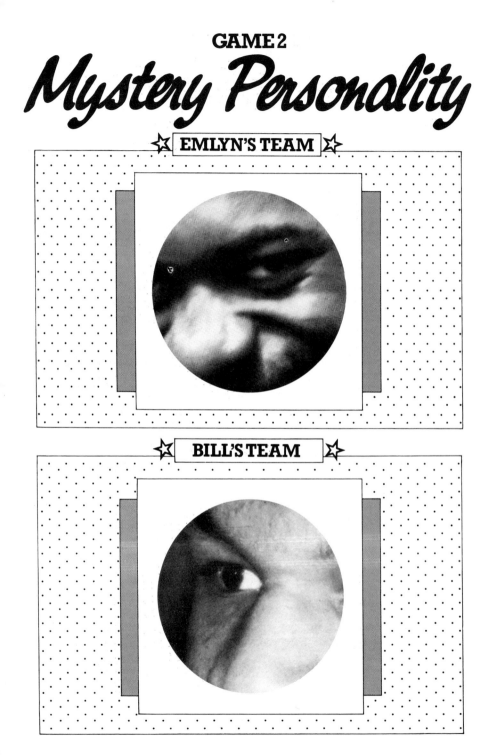

☆ **EMLYN'S TEAM** ☆

☆ **BILL'S TEAM** ☆

GAME 2
ANSWERS

PICTUREBOARD

1 Tessa Sanderson, Olympic javelin gold medallist in Los Angeles.
2 Jocky Wilson, christened John Thomas Wilson. Scotland's world darts champion in 1982 when he beat John Lowe in the final.
3 John Conteh, Britain's WBC world light-heavyweight boxing champion in 1974.
4 Brian McClair, Manchester United and Scotland striker—moved south from Celtic in 1987.

HOME & AWAY

JUDY (HOME)
East Germany.

(AWAY)
American football. They handle the measuring chain which determines whether or not a side has gained enough yardage for a 'down'.

LLOYD (HOME)
Colin Jones. He fought a draw in March 1983, and lost on points in the rematch five months later.

(AWAY)
A dead heat, unequalled before or since.

ERIC (HOME)
Leighton Rees. The Welshman has also captained his country, and last season (1987) was close on 60 caps.

(AWAY)
Wrestling. These are all various forms of the sport—and it's known in Iceland as Glima.

PETER (HOME)
1979—beat Malmo 1-0.
1980—beat SV Hamburg 1-0.

(AWAY)
Cyclo cross. The former is the most important event in the south of England, the latter is a facetiously titled informal competition.

EMLYN (HOME)
A 1000 lb German WWII bomb was found 100 yards from the ground. It took three days to defuse, and over 200 houses were evacuated. United won the delayed match 2–0.

(AWAY)
Fencing.

BILL (HOME)
Jim Aitken. It was Scotland's first Triple Crown in 46 years.

(AWAY)
Slobodan Zivojinovic. In ten years up to 1985 they were all unseeded players who reached the men's singles semi-finals at Wimbledon. Some became winners too!

ONE-MINUTE ROUND

EMLYN'S TEAM
1 Worcestershire.
2 John Lowe.
3 Tessa Sanderson.
4 Greg Lemond.
5 Brian Fletcher—1973/75.
Tommy Stack—1977.
6 a) Ray Train   b) Bill Lawrie   c) Franz Carr.

BILL'S TEAM
1 Phil Orr (playing in his 51st international against Romania for Ireland).
2 Welterweight.
3 Spurs (1984).
4 Eleven.
5 Silverstone and Aintree.
6 a) Phil Tuck   b) David Pleat   c) Neal Foulds.

MYSTERY PERSONALITY

EMLYN'S TEAM   Ben Johnson, the Canadian sprinter who became the fastest man over 100 m at the 1987 world championships in Rome.
BILL'S TEAM   Mike Tyson, the undisputed heavyweight boxing champion of the world.

GAME 3

Steve Davis takes slightly longer to score than Ian Rush, though both are at the top of their game. For this game Ian joins Bill's team along with Colin Deans from Scotland, whilst Steve teams up with 400 m champion Roger Black to talk Emlyn through the quiz.

✠ BILL'S TEAM ✠

COLIN DEANS Captain of Scotland in 1986. The most-capped hooker in their history, a member of the 1984 Grand Slam side, a British Lion, and a former skipper of the Barbarians. Problem is he has trouble recognising other Scottish international rugby players when they appear on the picture board, and pleaded with the editor to cut that section out of the programme. No can do! Sorry, Colin.

IAN RUSH In a seven-year spell with Liverpool Ian scored over 200 goals, won every domestic honour and a European Champions medal. Currently taking a package tour in Turin. Plays his international football for Wales, and lists his main hobby as clay pigeon shooting ('. . . and I sometimes miss.'). Claimed a hat-trick after getting three questions right on the show.

✠ EMLYN'S TEAM ✠

ROGER BLACK Sprang to prominence in the European Championships in 1986, where he was a double gold medallist with individual and relay 400 m victories. He'd already done exactly the same at the Commonwealth Games in Edinburgh. Roger is highly rated at spotting the Mystery Personality—all he has to do in this show is persuade Emlyn and Steve Davis to believe him.

STEVE DAVIS Has dominated snooker in the 80s, winning every major title, with his first world crown back in 1981. Despite appearances, has a great sense of humour and a wide-ranging love of music. Like Nigel Mansell bangs his head on the desk when he gets an answer wrong, but loves the programme enough to get out of a hotel bed in Preston and travel to the studios to cover for Kenny Sansom who was taken ill suddenly.

Pictureboard

GAME 3

Home & Away

COLIN
Who did Ciaran Fitzgerald succeed as captain of the Irish Rugby Union side?

In winning the British Grand Prix two years running, Nigel Mansell equalled the achievement of another Briton 21 years earlier—but who?

ROGER
Helsinki staged the 1983 World Athletics Championships. Name the Jamaican athlete who won the men's 400 m final.

In which sport are blue and black always partners against red and yellow?

IAN
With which club was John Aldridge top scorer before moving to Liverpool?

In which event did seven shoes and a sock bring Great Britain a gold medal in the 1986 European Athletic Championships?

STEVE
Which Welshman did Cliff Thorburn beat to win the 1985 Masters tournament at Wembley?

In which sport is the only obstacle 3 ft 6 in high?

BILL
England's pool in the first rugby union World Cup included Australia and the USA. Name the fourth country that made up the group.

Yachting: the 12-metre World Championships of 1987 was won by *New Zealand* representing New Zealand— but which country did runner-up *Bengal* represent?

EMLYN
Which English League club signed Danish international Allan Simonsen in 1982?

In greyhound racing in Britain what colour (or colours) are worn by the dog in trap two?

One-Minute Round

☆ BILL'S TEAM ☆

1 (1 pt)   Rugby: which was the last side to record a hat-trick of Scottish *club* championships?

•

2 (1 pt)   Soccer: for which European side did Glen Hoddle leave Spurs?

•

3 (1 pt)   Golf: who won his sixth US Masters title in 1986?

•

4 (1 pt)   Rugby: only one country has never lost all four matches during the International Championship season—which?

•

5 (2 pts)   Cricket: which two sides contested the 1987 Benson and Hedges final?

•

6 (3 pts)   Their surnames sound like drinks—complete them:
a) Athletics: Klaus (?)
b) Soccer: Mickey (?)
c) Eventing: Richard (?)

•

1 (1 pt)   Soccer: which club was the first winner of the League Cup?

2 (1 pt)   Athletics: name the Briton who reached the men's 400 m final in the 1980 Moscow Olympics.

3 (1 pt)   Cricket: which country toured England in the summer of '87?

4 (1 pt)   Snooker: who, in 1982, was the last Welshman to appear in the final of the World Championship?

5 (2 pts)   Rugby: which two players formed Scotland's record-breaking half-back partnership?

6 (3 pts)   Their surnames are also things you'd find in the kitchen:

     a) Racing: Michael (?)

     b) Cricket: Jack (?)

     c) Tennis: Betty (?)

GAME 3
Mystery Personality

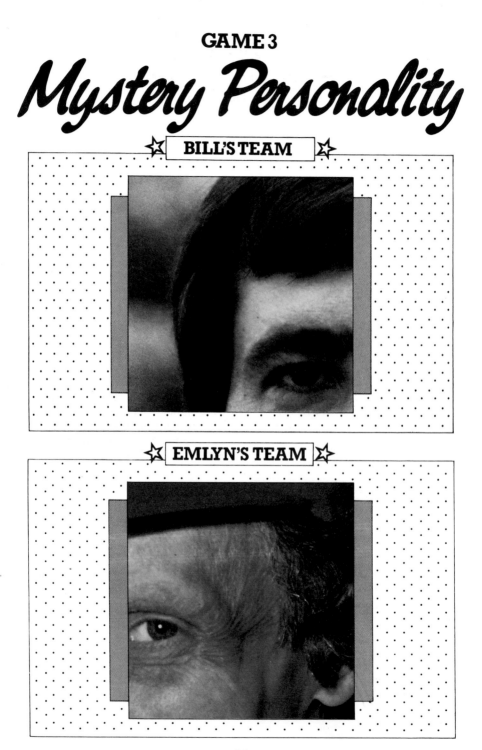

☆ BILL'S TEAM ☆

☆ EMLYN'S TEAM ☆

GAME 3
ANSWERS

PICTUREBOARD

1 Brendan Moon, a member of Australia's first ever rugby union Grand Slam tourists in 1984.
2 Glenn Hoddle, England midfield player, recently moved to Monaco after 12 years with Tottenham Hotspur.
3 Thomas Schoenlebe, East Germany's 400 m gold medallist in the 1987 World Athletics Championships in Rome.
4 Kirk Stevens, the Canadian snooker star, one of the few to have made a 147 break on television.

HOME & AWAY

COLIN (HOME)
Fergus Slattery. His last match was in March 1981. Fitzgerald took over and led Ireland to the Triple Crown in 1982.

(AWAY)
Jim Clark. In fact he won it five times between 1962-67—a record—with the first four wins consecutive. World champion twice in '63 and '65.

ROGER (HOME)
Bert Cameron. The Americans Mike Franks and Sunder Nix had to settle for silver and bronze.

(AWAY)
Croquet.

IAN (HOME)
Oxford United. Top scorer with Newport in 1983/84, and with Oxford the following two seasons before moving to Merseyside.

(AWAY)
The men's 4 × 400 m. Third string Brian Whittle lost his shoe on the changeover from Kriss Akabussi, but GB took the gold ahead of West Germany and the USSR.

STEVE (HOME)
Doug Mountjoy, winning by 9 frames to 6.

(AWAY)
Singles tennis: 3 ft 6 in is the height of the net.

BILL (HOME) (AWAY)
Japan. The Cup was won by the Australia.
New Zealand All Blacks, beating
France in the final.

EMLYN (HOME) (AWAY)
Charlton Athletic. Signed from Blue.
Barcelona—played only 16 games,
but scored 9 goals.

ONE-MINUTE ROUND

BILL'S TEAM
1 Hawick 1983/84; 1984/85; 1985/86.
2 Monaco.
3 Jack Nicklaus, and 6 wins is a record.
4 Wales.
5 Yorkshire and Northamptonshire. Yorkshire were the victors.
6 a) Klaus Beer   b) Mickey Gynn   c) Richard Meade.

EMLYN'S TEAM
1 Aston Villa, beating Rotherham over two legs.
2 David Jenkins.
3 Pakistan.
4 Ray Reardon, beaten 18–15 by Alex Higgins.
5 John Rutherford and Roy Laidlaw.
6 a) Michael Kettle   b) Jack Hobbs   c) Betty Stove.

MYSTERY PERSONALITY

BILL'S TEAM   Seve Ballesteros, the Spanish golfer who was a member of
the European team that won the Ryder Cup in 1985 and retained it in 1987.
EMLYN'S TEAM   Nikki Lauda, the indomitable Austrian who has won
the World Motor Racing Championship on three occasions.

GAME 4

Emlyn's called on overseas help for this game, with Hana Mandlikova joining him, and from golf Sam Torrance. To counter whatever Emlyn might know about soccer, Bill has Charlie Nicholas on his side, and given Em's second love—racing—he also has National Hunt jockey Peter Scudamore.

☆ BILL'S TEAM ☆

CHARLIE NICHOLAS Judged to be worth three-quarters of a million pounds when Arsenal brought him south from Celtic—not bad for a former motor mechanic. 'The Cannonball Kid' hit 48 goals in his last season in Glasgow. He doesn't mind the playboy image he's since developed, but won't admit to having Annabel's, Stringfellows, and the Hippodrome amongst his former clubs! Has boots, will travel.

PETER SCUDAMORE Said he'd much rather face Becher's Brook than the questions David Coleman asks—but one of the most knowledgeable guests to appear on the show. Shared the National Hunt championship with Johnny Francome in 1982, but went on to win it outright later.

☆ EMLYN'S TEAM ☆

HANA MANDLIKOVA Her first major success was winning the Australian title in 1980, and she has since won major tennis tournaments all round the world. Firmly set in the world's top five singles players, and broke the Evert/Navratilova dominance of the US Open with her win in 1985. On her first visit to the show asked for a transfer to Bill's team after two rounds with Emlyn—but has come back for a second look!

SAM TORRANCE Will long be remembered for sinking the putt in the 1985 Ryder Cup match that clinched that first European victory over the mighty Americans. The Scotsman has long been amongst the top players on the European circuit, with major tournament victories to his credit—though he's yet to achieve the big one of an Open title. Has been known to be 'well out of bounds' on the picture board. Gets on well with Em.

33

GAME 4
Pictureboard

1

2

3

4

GAME 4

Home & Away

CHARLIE
Which was the last club to win the Scottish FA Cup three years running (and it wasn't Celtic or Rangers)?

For a point apiece, what are the opening and closing events in the decathlon?

HANA
Navratilova's bid for a Grand Slam in 1984 came to a halt in the semi-finals of the Australian Open. Who was the Czech girl who stopped her?

What mustn't be less than 186 miles or more than 198.8 miles—and in any event must not go on for more than two hours?

PETER
The National Hunt record for consecutive wins is ten, set in 1959. Who equalled it in September 1986?

His birth name was Joe Sholto Douglas, but under which name did he write his way into the record books?

SAM
On which course did Nick Faldo win the 1987 Open?

Although best known for his baby-care books, Dr Benjamin Spock was an Olympic gold medallist. In what sport?

BILL
Originally it was known as the 'Australian Dispensation'—but what did it prevent players from doing?

In which major sporting event did Stephen Roche make his name in 1987?

EMLYN
Like you, Emlyn, he captained England, and could count amongst his clubs, Rotherham, Sunderland, Manchester City, Werder Bremen, Southampton and Fort Lauderdale. Who is he?

If a 'safety' costs you two points, what's the game?

One-Minute Round

1 (1 pt)   Soccer: which was the last side before Liverpool to retain the League Championship?

●

2 (1 pt)   Tennis: name the Australian girl who was Wimbledon ladies singles champion in 1980.

●

3 (1 pt)   Golf: who was the last golfer to win the Open at St Andrews twice?

●

4 (1 pt)   Snooker: who was the beaten finalist in the 1987 World Final?

●

5 (2 pts)   Athletics: in which two track events did Kratochvilova of Czechoslovakia win gold medals in the 1983 World Championships in Helsinki?

●

6 (3 pts)   Sports men and women who share their names with countries around the world. Complete them:

a) Soccer: Alan (?)

b) Tennis: Kathy (?)

c) Cricket: Bob (?)

●

1 (1 pt)   Rugby: against which country did Terry Holmes make his last appearance for Wales?

●

2 (1 pt)   Racing: which horse did Steve Knight ride to victory in the 1987 Grand National?

●

3 (1 pt)   Soccer: when playing in the First Division Ian Rush failed to score against only one club. Which one?

●

4 (1 pt)   In which sport is Norman Dagley a world champion?

●

5 (2 pts)   Athletics: in which two track events did British girls win silver medals at the Los Angeles Olympics in 1984?

●

6 (3 pts)   Their surnames you might find when out walking. What are they?

   a) Soccer: Greg (?)

   b) Racing: Richard (?)

   c) Cricket: Bobby (?)

●

GAME 4
Mystery Personality

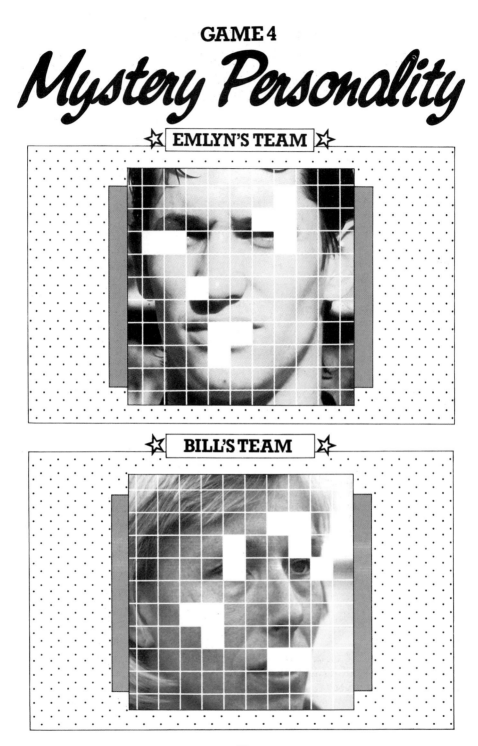

GAME 4 ANSWERS

PICTUREBOARD

1 Steffi Graf, West Germany's tennis star who won her first Grand Slam tournament in Paris in 1987, and is poised to take over from Martina Navratilova as the world's number one player.

2 Paul Way, British golfer who won the 1987 European Open at Walton Heath.

3 Richard Gough, the ex-Spurs captain, returned north of the border to join Glasgow Rangers in a deal which made him the most expensive buy in Scottish football.

4 John Francome, National Hunt jockey on no less than six occasions and earning a reputation as a writer.

HOME & AWAY

CHARLIE (HOME)
Aberdeen, winning in 1982/3/4. They beat Rangers on the first two occasions, Celtic on the third.

(AWAY)
The 100 m sprint and the 1500 m.

HANA (HOME)
Helena Sukova. Sukova suffered a three-set defeat in the final against Chris Evert-Lloyd.

(AWAY)
A Formula One Grand Prix race—ask Nigel Mansell!

PETER (HOME)
Phil Tuck. Doronicum was his 10th winner at Southall in September 1986—coincidentally the same month the record was set 27 years earlier.

(AWAY)
The Marquis of Queensberry, lending his patronage to the work of Lord Lonsdale and Arthur Chambers, who in 1867 drafted the rules of boxing as we know them today.

SAM (HOME)
Muirfield, winning by one stroke from America's Paul Azinger and Australia's Rodger Davis.

(AWAY)
Rowing—he was a member of the USA Eights crew which won the gold medal in Paris in 1924.

BILL (HOME)
It stopped rugby union players kicking the ball directly into touch, other than from within their own 22-metre line.

(AWAY)
The Tour de France. He made his name by winning the race—and becoming the first British Isles rider to do so.

EMLYN (HOME)
Dave Watson. Not to be confused with the Dave Watson of Everton.

(AWAY)
American grid-iron football. If you are caught in possession inside your own 'end zone' the opposition collects two points.

ONE-MINUTE ROUND

EMLYN'S TEAM
1 Wolves, in the 1958/59 season: their third title.
2 Evonne Cawley (née Goolagong). It was her second title, having won in 1971.
3 Jack Nicklaus, winning in both 1970 and 1978.
4 Joe Johnson. Then the defending champion, he lost to Steve Davis.
5 The 400 m and the 800 m.
6 a) Alan Brazil   b) Kathy Jordan   c) Bob Holland.

BILL'S TEAM
1 Fiji. In November 1985, he captained the side and scored a try, and Wales won 40–3.
2 Maori Venture.
3 Manchester United.
4 Billiards.
5 The 100 m hurdles and 3000 m (Shirley Strong and Wendy Sly).
6 a) Greg Downs   b) Richard Hills   c) Bobby Parks.

MYSTERY PERSONALITY

EMLYN'S TEAM   Gary Lineker, the England striker who left Everton for Barcelona.
BILL'S TEAM   Martina Navratilova, winner of the Wimbledon ladies singles titles on the last six occasions, and for many years the undisputed number one in the world.

GAME 5

Two world champions have turned up for this game, one on two legs, the other on four. World eventing champion Ginny Leng partners England rugby union captain Mike Harrison on Bill's side, whilst boxing world title holder Terry Marsh and Irish international David O'Leary will be helping Emlyn.

✕ BILL'S TEAM ✕

VIRGINIA LENG A gutsy lady who nearly lost an arm in a riding accident in 1977, but went on to win the World three-day event title in Australia in 1986. Has also won at Burghley and Badminton, and the European Championships. When not on Priceless or Nightcap, she likes skiing, collecting antiques, reading, and embarrassing Bill. Last time on the show she insisted the answer to 'What Happened Next?' was: 'He got hit in the . . .!'

MIKE HARRISON Mike looked destined to become captain for his country when he ran virtually the length of the field on his debut to score a try for England against New Zealand in 1985. He led the England XV in the inaugural rugby union World Cup 'down under', scoring five tries (a performance bettered only by two other players during the tournament). Was intercepted by Bill when he tried to smuggle a *Rugby World* magazine on to the set.

✕ EMLYN'S TEAM ✕

DAVID O'LEARY The Republic of Ireland international who has over 750 appearances for Arsenal to his credit, including successive Cup Finals in 1978, '79 and '80. Though born in London he spent his childhood in Dublin with brother Pierce, who has also partnered him in the Eire side. Became the first guest to sing on the show when he led a chorus of 'Here We Go' after a dramatic win in Emlyn's team. Can he repeat it?

TERRY MARSH Ex-Royal Marine, who retired as undefeated world light-welterweight champion in 1987, and who is probably the most famous fireman in the world. Turned professional boxer as recently as 1981, became British champion, then European, and ultimately world title holder when he beat Joe Manley in 1987. After David Coleman's introduction he charged into the television studio with a fire hose, and had to be restrained from turning it on the audience—some fireman!

GAME 5
Pictureboard

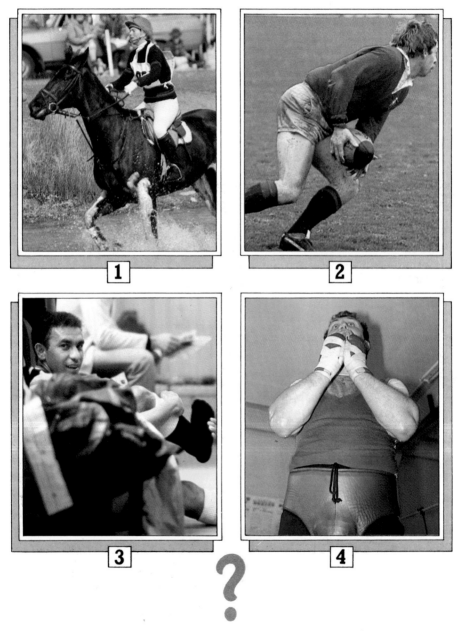

1

2

3

4

?

Home & Away

VIRGINIA
On which horse did Captain Mark Phillips record his third Badminton win in 1981?

How many consecutive shots must be taken to complete a total clearance of a snooker table?

DAVID
Against which club did Scarborough make their Football League debut?

What sport would you be watching if a fireman came on as relief?

MIKE
Wales recorded three Grand Slam wins in the 1970s with three different captains. It was John Dawes in 1971 and Phil Bennett in 1978. Who was the captain in 1976?

In which sport was Greg Louganis of the USA a double gold medallist in the 1984 Olympic Games?

TERRY
Wilfredo Benitez held world titles at both welterweight and light-welterweight. What was his nationality?

Barbecue and Sunset are two right-hand bends you'd take before reaching the club-house—on which Grand Prix circuit would you find them?

BILL
If the Royal Navy have just won the Stewart Wrightson Trophy, which is the only side they could have beaten?

Who was on 'Full Choke' for his final win?

EMLYN
Which Scottish club did Frank McAvennie leave to join West Ham United?

This sport was invented in 1918 by a Swedish army major, based on the military exercises of the 1890s. The largest number of competitors in any one event stands at 22,510. What's the sport?

One-Minute Round

☆ BILL'S TEAM ☆

1 (1 pt) Rugby: which Welsh fly-half captained the British Lions on their 1977 tour to New Zealand and Fiji?

•

2 (1 pt) Eventing: who rode Charisma to become his country's first gold medallist in the 1984 Olympics?

•

3 (1 pt) Athletics: to which athletics club does Linford Christie belong?

•

4 (1 pt) Rugby: which country did Jim Aitken captain to a Grand Slam in the season 1983/84?

•

5 (2 pts) Who's the only British water-skier to have won the overall men's world title?

•

6 (3 pts) The missing names could also be items of clothing.
  a) Soccer: Kenny (?)
  b) Cricket: (?) Connor
  c) Athletics: Geoff (?)

•

☆ EMLYN'S TEAM ☆

1 (1 pt)   Soccer: with which League side did Bobby Charlton finish his playing career?

2 (1 pt)   Boxing: at which weight did Clinton McKenzie win a European title in 1981?

3 (1 pt)   Cricket: in the MCC Bicentenary match at Lord's in August 1987 what did Gooch, Gower, Gatting and Gavaskar have in common?

4 (1 pt)   Which was the first British football club to win the European Cup?

5 (2 pts)   Who did the New York Giants beat to win the 1987 American Football Superbowl?

6 (3 pts)   They're furry animals, as well as sportsmen. Name them.
a) Golf: Hew (?)
b) Canoeing: Richard (?)
c) Rugby: Kieran (?)

GAME 5
Mystery Personality

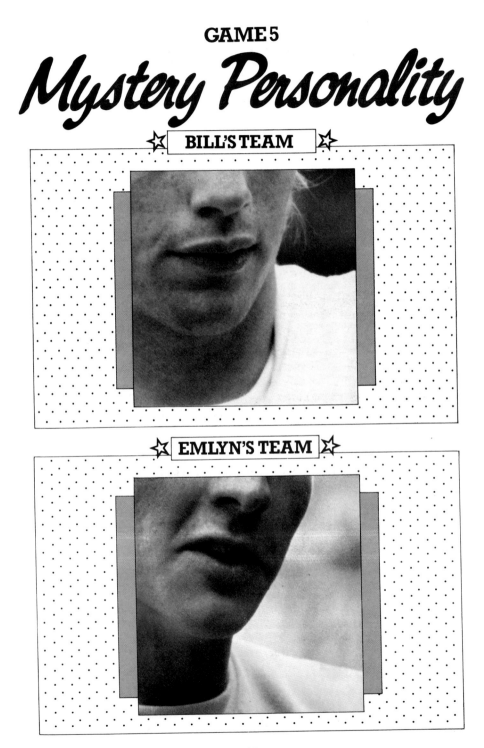

☆ **BILL'S TEAM** ☆

☆ **EMLYN'S TEAM** ☆

GAME 5
ANSWERS

PICTUREBOARD

1 Diana Clapham, the eventer who was a member of the 1984 Olympic silver medal-winning team on her horse Windjammer.

2. Roy Laidlaw, of Selkirk and Scotland. He holds the record for most caps ever at scrum-half, and for the world's most capped half-back partnership with John Rutherford.

3 Mirandinha, Brazilian striker who joined Newcastle United from Sao Paulo's Palmeras for £600,000 in August 1987.

4 Joe Bugner, the former British heavyweight boxing champion, now a naturalised Australian. He went the distance with Muhammad Ali in 1975.

HOME & AWAY

VIRGINIA (HOME)
Lincoln. His first two wins came in 1971 and 1972 on Great Ovation.

(AWAY)
36. 15 reds, each followed by a colour—making 30—plus the six colours themselves.

DAVID (HOME)
Wolverhampton Wanderers. The result: a 2–2 draw.

(AWAY) .
Baseball. The 'fireman' is the American term for the man who comes on as relief pitcher.

MIKE (HOME)
Mervyn Davies.

(AWAY)
Diving. He won both the platform and springboard gold medals.

TERRY (HOME)
American. In 1976 he was WBA Light-welterweight champion, in 1979 WBC Welterweight champion. And in 1981 he became WBA Light-middleweight champion too!

(AWAY)
Kyalami. They are sections of the Formula One Grand Prix circuit which now stages the South African Grand Prix.

BILL (HOME)
The Army. The trophy is contested annually between the two services, and the match is played at Twickenham.

(AWAY)
Lester Piggott, at Colwick Park, Nottingham. Full Choke was his 4349th winner, including 29 Classic victories and 9 Derby wins.

EMLYN (HOME)
St Mirren, signing for £340,000.

(AWAY)
Orienteering. Using map and compass and a given route, competitors are required to finish the course in as short a time as possible, checking in at staging posts along the way.

ONE-MINUTE ROUND

BILL'S TEAM
1 Phil Bennett.
2 Mark Todd of New Zealand.
3 Thames Valley Harriers.
4 Scotland.
5 Mike Hazlewood, in 1977.
6 a) Kenny Jackett   b) Cardigan Connor   c) Geoff Capes.

EMLYN'S TEAM
1 Preston North End. He played 38 games in the season 1974/75, scoring 8 goals. In 604 League games for Manchester United—his only other club as a player—Bobby scored 198 goals.
2 Light-welterweight.
3 The four G's all scored centuries—and were the only players to do so.
4 Celtic.
5 Denver Broncos.
6 a) Hew Squirrell   b) Richard Fox   c) Kieran Rabbit.

MYSTERY PERSONALITY

BILL'S TEAM   Boris Becker, the West German tennis star who became the youngest player ever to win the Wimbledon title at the age of 17 in 1985.
EMLYN'S TEAM   Steve Cram, one of the greatest middle distance runners of all time. World champion over 1500 m in 1983 and several times world record holder at a variety of middle distances.

GAME 6

Lucinda Green, former world champion and one of the show's biggest fans, joins forces with England cricket captain Mike Gatting and Bill for this one. Meanwhile Emlyn, with a view to getting his soccer questions right, has Everton's Trevor Steven on his team, with support from tennis star Peter Fleming.

☆ BILL'S TEAM ☆

MIKE GATTING Took over the England captaincy in 1986, and returned from the Australian tour with every pot going—including the Ashes. A courageous batsman: remember his smashed nose on the West Indies tour? Also captain of Middlesex, Mike once hit 207 in Madras against India, but commented that if you can't get the runs in India you can't get them anywhere! Bill's expecting a good fielding performance from him when the questions get hot.

LUCINDA GREEN The former world three-day event riding champion controls both Emlyn and Bill as well as she does her horses, but her no-nonsense approach is coupled with a great sense of fun. Has won every honour in a tough sport—Burghley, Badminton, European Individual champion, and champion of the world. Has also helped the British team to European and World team titles. Looking for a clear round with Bill.

☆ EMLYN'S TEAM ☆

TREVOR STEVEN Everton midfielder who's already collected two League Championship medals, an FA Cup winners medal, and a European Cup Winners Cup medal! To add to that he joined England for the World Cup Finals in Mexico. Quite how he's going to fare
with former Liverpool skipper Emlyn we'll see—but Bill has offered to put in a transfer bid when his contract runs out.

PETER FLEMING Formed one half of the world-famous doubles partnership with John McEnroe, with whom he won four Wimbledon titles, three US Open titles, and seven US Masters championships, as well as Davis Cup success. Asked if he thought Emlyn was a good captain, came back with the immortal remark: 'You cannot be serious!'

Pictureboard

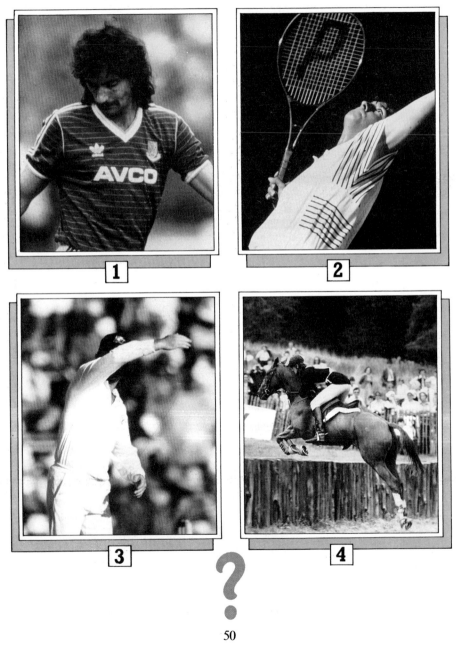

1

2

3

4

GAME 6

Home & Away

TREVOR
Which Midlands' First Division side did Altrincham knock out of the 1985/86 FA Cup?

Motor Racing: the first British Grand Prix (then called the RAC Grand Prix) was staged in 1926. On which circuit was it held?

MIKE
Against which country does England contest the Wisden Trophy?

With which sport do you associate the former Hungarian acrobat Joe Turi?

PETER
Which all-Australian men's pair won the Wimbledon doubles title in 1982?

Who was the only Indian cricketer to appear in the MCC side for the Bicentenary match at Lord's in '87?

LUCINDA
When Ginny Leng won the world title on Priceless in Australia in 1986, a British lady took the bronze on Mycross—name her.

His father was a singer, his mother an actress, his sister shot JR and he was the 1981 US amateur golf champion. Out of the riddle can you name the family?

EMLYN
Which player left Brazilian club Palmeiras in August '87 to play English League football?

Why were the people of Nottingham celebrating 11 sixes in 1981?

BILL
Which player captained the French side to a Grand Slam in the 70s, and then coached them to the same success in the 80s?

In which sport did Janet Evans break two world records in 1987?

GAME 6
One-Minute Round

1 (1 pt)   Soccer: who were the last side to retain the FA Cup?

2 (1 pt)   When will the Summer Olympics next be held in Europe?

3 (1 pt)   Which famous sporting venue will you find on Harleyford Road?

4 (1 pt)   Tennis: who was the last Frenchman to win the French Open in 1983?

5 (2 pts)   Soccer: who marked his debut for Arsenal with a goal against Liverpool in the 1985/86 season?

6 (3 pts)   Their names are also international currencies— complete them.
a) Cricket: Vic (?)
b) Athletics: Mary (?)
c) Golf: Bob (?)

1 (1 pt) Rugby: which country did New Zealand play in the opening match of the inaugural World Cup in '87?

●

2 (1 pt) Cricket: who set a Sunday League record of 13 sixes in an innings in 1986?

●

3 (1 pt) Tennis: where are the US Open Championships staged?

●

4 (1 pt) Eventing: who had his only success at Burghley with Maid Marion?

●

5 (2 pts) Soccer: which club were FA Cup Finalists in 1983—and were relegated the same season?

●

6 (3 pts) Their surnames would all be associated with still or running water—who are they?

a) Rallying: Tony (?)

b) Tennis: Johann (?)

c) Rugby: Zinzan (?)

●

GAME 6
Mystery Personality

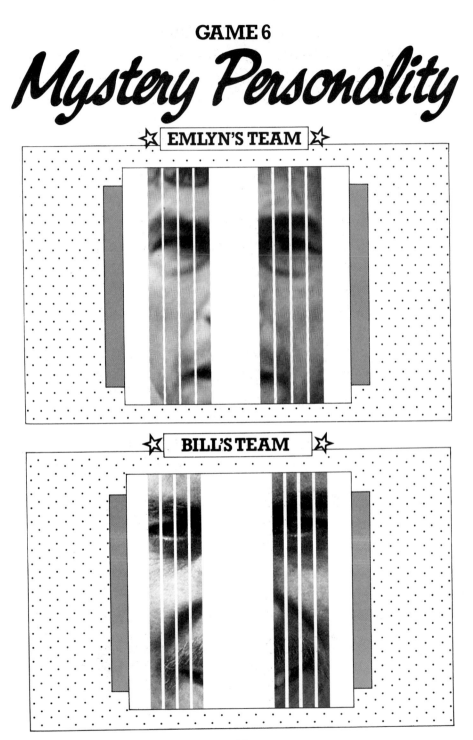

☆ **EMLYN'S TEAM** ☆

☆ **BILL'S TEAM** ☆

GAME 6
ANSWERS

1 Alan Devonshire, West Ham and England midfield player with over 300 League appearances for the Upton Park side.
2 Gabriela Sabatini, Argentinian tennis star ranked world number one junior in 1984, now amongst the world's top ten ladies.
3 Allan Border, the Australian Test cricket captain.
4 Mark Todd, the New Zealander who won the 1984 three-day event. He is seen here riding Jocasta.

HOME & AWAY

TREVOR (HOME)
Birmingham City. Altrincham won 2–1 in the third round at St Andrews—but were themselves beaten 2–0 in the next round by York City.

(AWAY)
Brooklands. The Surrey track also staged the race the following year. The event was to become the British Grand Prix in 1949.

MIKE (HOME)
West Indies. It was first contested in 1963. England have only won it twice--under Colin Cowdrey in 1967/68, and Ray Illingworth in 1969.

(AWAY)
Showjumping. He was a double winner at Hickstead in 1987 on Vital and Kruger.

PETER (HOME)
Peter McNamara and Paul McNamee. It was their second Wimbledon title.

(AWAY)
Ravi Shastri.

LUCINDA (HOME)
Lorna Clarke. She also won a team gold with the British squad.

(AWAY)
Crosby. Bing's son, Nathaniel, was no mean golfer—and the rest of the family's successes are well documented.

EMLYN (HOME)
Mirandinha, joining Newcastle in a £600,000 move.

(AWAY)
Jayne Torvill and Christopher Dean recorded eleven perfect scores on their way to becoming European champions.

BILL (HOME)
Jacques Fouroux. He captained France in 1977, and was coach to the side in 1981 and 1987. Each year was a French Grand Slam.

(AWAY)
Swimming. She broke world records at both 800 m and 1500 m freestyle at the US National Long Course Championships in California.

ONE-MINUTE ROUND

EMLYN'S TEAM
1 Spurs in 1981 and 1982, beating Manchester City and QPR with both matches going to a replay.
2 1992 in Barcelona, Spain.
3 The Oval, home of Surrey County Cricket Club.
4 Yannick Noah, beating Mats Wilander in straight sets.
5 Niall Quinn in December 1985 at Highbury—Arsenal won 2–0.
6 a) Vic Marks   b) Mary Rand   c) Bob Gilder.

BILL'S TEAM
1 Italy. New Zealand won 70–6! They went on to become the first World Champions and were unbeaten.
2 Ian Botham, then with Somerset. He was 175 not out, and also hit 12 fours.
3 Flushing Meadow on the outskirts of New York.
4 Captain Mark Phillips. In 1973.
5 Brighton.They lost the final 4–0 to Manchester United in the replay following a 2–2 draw in the first game.
6 a) Tony Pond   b) Johann Kriek   c) Zinzan Brooke.

MYSTERY PERSONALITY

EMLYN'S TEAM   Imran Khan, Pakistan's cricket captain. One of the few men to have taken over 300 Test wickets.
BILL'S TEAM   Kenny Sansom, the Arsenal skipper. He has played for England in two World Cups.

Emlyn's sparring partner for this game is heavyweight Frank
Bruno, with England fly-half Rob Andrew joining in to provide
the deft touches. Bill counters with England defender Terry
Butcher, and Commonwealth gold medallist over 10,000 metres,
Liz Lynch.

☆ BILL'S TEAM ☆

TERRY BUTCHER Born in Singapore, but managed
to make his way to England in time to become one of
the mainstays of the England team, playing in the
World Cup Finals in both Spain and Mexico. After ten
years with Ipswich he joined Glasgow Rangers in 1986,
and was hailed as one of their heroes when the Ibrox
team took the Scottish Championship. Watch for the
clenched fist salute when he gets his soccer questions
right!

LIZ LYNCH Liz really set a first when she ran to the
studios for her debut on *A Question of Sport*—though
she did come from a city centre hotel, and not her home
town of Dundee! Athletics questions didn't bother her:
she really knew her stuff. And all Scotland cheered her
home when she won the 10,000 metres Commonwealth
gold medal in Edinburgh in the summer of '86.

☆ EMLYN'S TEAM ☆

FRANK BRUNO European heavyweight champion in
1985, and still Britain's major hope for a world title bid.
A great favourite with the British public. On one show
he was stalling for time on his question when Emlyn
finally passed him a note. It read: 'You're on your own,
pal.' Emlyn must be either brave or daft—and probably
the latter.

ROB ANDREW England's stylish fly-half, who scored
eighteen points out of twenty-two on his international
debut against Rumania in 1985. Should be good on the
questions after his years of studying at Cambridge Uni-
versity. However, he'll long be remembered for his
'Mystery Personality' appearance when he agreed to
take a shower—wearing a frogman's outfit. Some sense
of humour, eh?

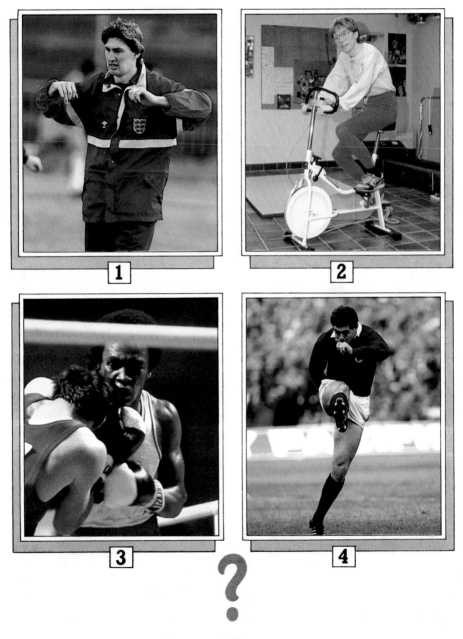

1

2

3

4

GAME 7

Home & Away

TERRY
Which London club appeared in successive FA Cup Finals in 1978, 1979 and 1980?

What's the lowest number you cannot score with a single dart?

FRANK
Who did Mike Tyson defeat to become undisputed heavyweight champion of the world?

In which sport have Jacques and Lewis been appointed to lead a British revival?

LIZ
Name the Norwegian girl who became the first European 10,000 m champion in 1986.

Which sport has a 'beach start' and a 'dock start'?

ROB
With 14 caps at centre and 22 caps on the wing who, between 1969 and 1976, became England's most-capped three-quarter?

Which Scottish championship golf course has Ailsa Craig lying offshore?

BILL
Between which two sides is the Bowring Bowl annually contested?

Which sport staged its European championship at Picketts Lock in 1987?

EMLYN
Which Italian club did Trevor Francis leave to join Rangers in the summer of 1987?

In which sport did Cameron and Waldo become world champions in Madrid in 1986?

One-Minute Round

☆ BILL'S TEAM ☆

1 (1 pt)   Rugby: for which Rugby League side did Welsh international Terry Holmes turn professional?

•

2 (1 pt)   Soccer: England's cricket captain Mike Gatting has a brother in professional football. For which club did he make an FA Cup Final appearance?

•

3 (1 pt)   Athletics: which girl was world cross country champion for the first time in 1985—and retained the title in 1986?

•

4 (1 pt)   Racing: in which Scottish city is Britain's newest National Hunt course?

•

5 (2 pts)   Cricket: which two countries staged the 1987 World Cup?

•

6 (3 pts)   Their surnames all sound like cereal crops—complete them:

     a) Athletics: James (?)

     b) Cricket: Clive (?)

     c) Rugby: Brian (?)

•

1 (1 pt) Soccer: where were the 1974 World Cup Finals staged?

2 (1 pt) Rugby: which East European country beat Scotland just two months after the Scottish Grand Slam of 1985?

3 (1 pt) Who was the only British-based boxer to go 15 rounds with Muhammad Ali?

4 (1 pt) With what sport would you associate 'The Powderhall'?

5 (2 pts) Snooker: who did Alex Higgins defeat in taking his two world titles?

6 (3 pts) You might say that they all have an ecclesiastical ring to their name . . . but complete them:
a) American football: Art (?)
b) Athletics: Glynnis (?)
c) Soccer: Owen (?)

GAME 7

Mystery Personality

GAME 7
ANSWERS

PICTUREBOARD

1 Tony Adams, the England and Arsenal defender.
2 Ingrid Kristiansen, Norway's 1987 women's world athletics champion for the 10,000 m.
3 Sugar Ray Leonard, America's world welterweight champion, now retired after defeating Marvin Hagler for the world middleweight crown.
4 Gavin Hastings, the older of the two Scottish rugby union international brothers. He scored 21 points, a record for a full back, against England at Murrayfield in 1986.

HOME & AWAY

TERRY (HOME)
Arsenal. They lost the first to Ipswich, beat Manchester United in the second, and lost the third to West Ham United.

(AWAY)
23.

FRANK (HOME)
Tony Tucker, the IBF world champion—Tyson beat him on points over 12 rounds in Las Vegas, August 1987.

(AWAY)
Tennis. Warren Jacques has become international squad director, and Richard Lewis takes up training and coaching.

LIZ (HOME)
Ingrid Kristiansen at Stuttgart in August 1986. She became the first woman in history to go under 31 mins—her time was 30:23.25.

(AWAY)
Water-skiing.

ROB (HOME)
David Duckham.

(AWAY)
Turnberry. Ailsa Craig also gives its name to the Ailsa Championship course.

BILL (HOME)
Oxford and Cambridge.

(AWAY)
Ladies hockey.

EMLYN (HOME)
Atalanta. Rangers' manager Graeme Souness paid £70,000 to bring him back after 5 years in Italy. Trevor's first club there was Sampdoria.

(AWAY)
Synchronised swimming: the Canadians became world pairs champions.

ONE-MINUTE ROUND

BILL'S TEAM
1 Bradford Northern.
2 Brighton in 1983.
3 Zola Budd.
4 Edinburgh.
5 Pakistan and India.
6 a) James Mays   b) Clive Rice   c) Brian Barley.

EMLYN'S TEAM
1 West Germany.
2 Romania, winning 28–22.
3 Joe Bugner, at Kuala Lumpur in July 1975.
4 Athletics: it is the top professional sprint race in Britain.
5 John Spencer in 1972; Ray Reardon in 1982.
6 a) Art Monk   b) Glynnis Nunn   c) Owen Archdeacon.

MYSTERY PERSONALITY

BILL'S TEAM   Barry McGuigan, the former world featherweight boxing champion from Northern Ireland.
EMLYN'S TEAM   Sebastian Coe, former Olympic champion at 1500 m and former world record holder for the 800 m, 1500 m and the mile.

GAME 8

Emlyn seems to be expecting another punch-up, with Herol 'Bomber' Graham in his team along with 5000-metre star Jack Buckner. But one might expect a more studied approach from Canada's former world snooker champion, Cliff Thorburn, who'll be helping Bill, with footballer Mark Lawrenson.

☆ BILL'S TEAM ☆

CLIFF THORBURN The Canadian who was snooker's first overseas world champion of modern times, winning in 1980. Went on to score the first maximum 147 break of the World Championship. That brought him to his knees—and so do the snooker questions fired at him by David Coleman, he says. Emlyn reckons that when he misses out it's four away—and he'll 'ave 'em!

MARK LAWRENSON Has won every honour in English football since signing for Liverpool from Brighton in 1981. Also played a major part in the club's success in Europe. England managers are often found scratching their heads about Preston-born Mark playing for the Republic of Ireland—they should blame his mum, and the fact they weren't in quick enough. However, Mark could be left head-scratching in this game.

☆ EMLYN'S TEAM ☆

JACK BUCKNER The 1986 Commonwealth Games 5000-metre silver medal winner who went on to win the European gold medal in Stuttgart later that year. A good man for the 'What Happened Next?' round with an imagination that impressed even Emlyn. Jack explained that he dreams up the answers whilst on the training track. So that's what he's thinking about as he goes round and round and round and round . . .

HEROL GRAHAM The only time Herol doesn't laugh is when he's in the ring, where he's made a hobby of collecting titles. He was undefeated British, Commonwealth and European light-middleweight champion when he moved up one class to become British and European middleweight champ. His fighting style earned him the nickname 'Bomber'. One problem—being next to Emlyn the pair of them ended up like a couple of laughing hyenas.

GAME 8
Pictureboard

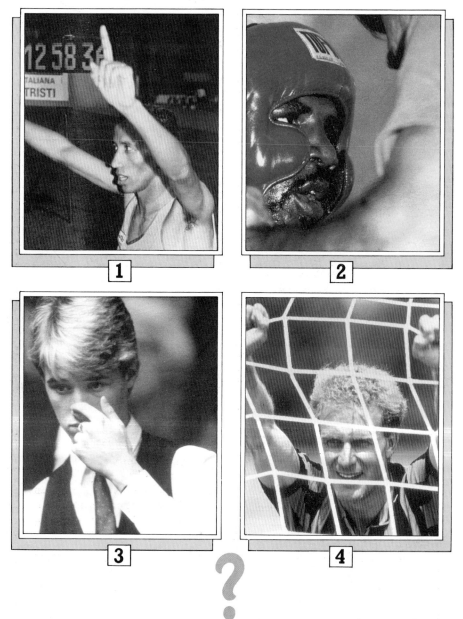

1

2

3

4

?

66

GAME 8

Home & Away

JACK
Which athlete, in 1978, broke world records at 3000 m, 5000 m, 10,000 m and the 3000 m steeplechase?

Little Brown Jug, Yonker's Futurity, and the Hambletonian are major events—but what's the sport?

CLIFF
Who did Steve Davis beat in 1986 for his fifth United Kingdom title?

Which Olympic sport has 12 players a side, two of them goalkeepers, allows only seven on court at any one time, and has two halves of 30 minutes?

HEROL
Which boxer, having won an Olympic middleweight gold medal in 1976, went on to win professional world titles at both light-heavyweight and heavyweight?

Which city staged the final of the 1987 cricket World Cup?

MARK
England scored seven goals in the World Cup in Mexico in 1986. Six came from Gary Lineker. Who scored the seventh?

If the Maple Leafs were playing the Saracens, which sport would you be watching in Britain?

EMLYN
Which club retained its First Division status in the first play-offs brought in, in 1987?

Which character from Shakespeare's *A Midsummer Night's Dream* shares his name with a piece of sporting equipment?

BILL
Which lock-forward collected 17 caps for the British Lions between 1962 and 1974, thereby setting a record?

Which major British sporting event has been won by an Anglo, a Russian Hero and a Wild Man of Borneo?

GAME 8
One-Minute Round

☆ EMLYN'S TEAM ☆

1 (1 pt) Soccer: name the first club promoted with more than 100 points in a season.

2 (1 pt) Snooker: what was Steve Davis' first major title?

3 (1 pt) Soccer: which goalkeeper played in successive League Cup finals for different teams in 1981 and 1982?

4 (1 pt) Tennis: which Australian achieved a hat-trick of titles at the 1970 US Open?

5 (2 pts) In which countries were the 1980 and 1984 Winter Olympics staged?

6 (3 pts) Their names are also parts of the body. Complete them.
   a) Racing: Freddie (?)
   b) Swimming: Joe (?)
   c) Soccer: Jim (?)

☆ BILL'S TEAM ☆

1 (1 pt) Rugby: which Frenchman holds the record for the most points in a championship season, with 54?

2 (1 pt) Athletics: which Irish athlete became world 5000 m champion at the 1983 Games staged in Helsinki?

3 (1 pt) Boxing: at which Olympic Games did Chris Finnegan take the middleweight gold medal?

4 (1 pt) In February 1987 New Delhi was the venue for a world championship. Name the sport.

5 (2 pts) Horse racing: Woodbine and Randwick are famous courses. In which countries would you find them?

6 (3 pts) They share their surnames with areas of London. Complete them.

  a) Soccer: John (?)

  b) Eventing: Diana (?)

  c) Athletics: Roger (?)

GAME 8

Mystery Personality

☆ **EMLYN'S TEAM** ☆

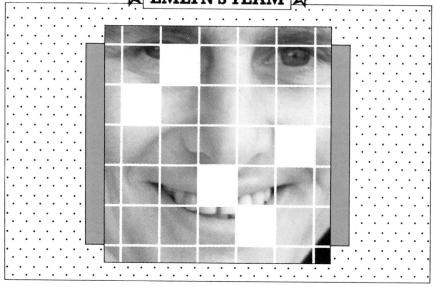

☆ **BILL'S TEAM** ☆

GAME 8
ANSWERS

PICTUREBOARD

1 Said Aouita, the Moroccan 'magician' who makes a habit of breaking world athletics records.
2 Marvin Hagler, 'Marvellous' Marvin, the former world middleweight boxing champion—a title he took from Alan Minter in London in 1980.
3 Stephen Hendry, the young Scottish snooker star, winner of the Rothmans Grand Prix in 1987 and tipped to be a future world champion.
4 Karl Heinz Rumenigger, the West German international who was European Footballer of the Year in 1981.

HOME & AWAY

JACK (HOME)
Henry Rono of Kenya.

(AWAY)
Harness racing or trotting. They are all major races on the calendar in the USA for trotters and pacers.

CLIFF (HOME)
Neal Foulds. Davis won by 16 frames to 7.

(AWAY)
Handball.

HEROL (HOME)
Michael Spinks. He became light-heavyweight world champion in 1981 and heavyweight world champion in 1985.

(AWAY)
Calcutta, at Eden Gardens. The tournament was staged at venues in both India and Pakistan.

MARK (HOME)
Peter Beardsley, scoring one of the goals in the 3-0 win over Paraguay.

(AWAY)
Polo. Both are amongst the leading polo teams in Britain: HRH the Prince of Wales is a member of the Maple Leafs.

EMLYN (HOME)
Charlton Athletic, beating Leeds United to stay up.

(AWAY)
Puck—the rubber disc used in ice hockey.

BILL (HOME)
Willie John McBride. He also
collected 63 caps for Ireland
between 1962 and 1975.

(AWAY)
The Grand National. They were
winners in 1966, 1949 and 1895
respectively.

ONE-MINUTE ROUND

EMLYN'S TEAM
1 York City. They gained 101 points in the season 1983–84, and were
promoted to Division Three.
2 UK 1980, beating Alex Higgins 16–6.
3 Ray Clemence, with Liverpool in 1981 and with Spurs in 1982.
4 Margaret Court.
5 USA (Lake Placid), 1980; Yugoslavia (Sarajevo), 1984.
6 a) Freddie Head   b) Joe Bottom   c) Jim Bone.

BILL'S TEAM
1 Jean-Pierre Lescarboura in the 1983–84 season with 10 penalty goals, 6
conversions, and 4 drop-goals.
2 Eamonn Coghlan.
3 The 1968 Games in Mexico City, winning on a split decision 3–2 against
Aleksei Kisselyov of the USSR.
4 Table tennis.
5 Canada (Woodbine); Australia (Randwick).
6 a) John Barnes   b) Diana Clapham   c) Roger Hackney.

MYSTERY PERSONALITY

BILL'S TEAM   Derek Warwick, the British Grand Prix motor racing
driver.
EMLYN'S TEAM   Willie Carson, one of Britain's leading jockeys on the fl.
and a winner of numerous classic races.

Both Bill and Emlyn have gone abroad for guests, Bill to France, where he found Scottish footballer Mo Johnston in voluntary exile, and Emlyn to Denmark, for world speedway champion Hans Nielsen. Bill's team is completed by jockey Walter Swinburn, and Emlyn's by England cricketer Chris Broad.

⭐ BILL'S TEAM ⭐

MO JOHNSTON Only in his mid-twenties, but much-travelled. Has proved a getter of goals north and south of the border, or, as at present, across the Channel with Nantes. Previously played for Partick Thistle, then Watford, where he got a losers medal in the 1984 Cup Final. Went one better 12 months later, with Celtic's Scottish FA Cup-winning team. Has been hoping that the French defenders he now meets have legs like frogs and run like snails!

WALTER SWINBURN Bill was really on to a winner with Walter's first showing. The diminutive jockey answered absolutely everything—soccer, rugby, cricket, the lot. But he's so used to winning—remember Shergar? Since then classic victories have become the norm, here and abroad. A sports nut that Emlyn's insisting he wants 'doped' before he comes on the programme again—or else he's on his team. 'No' is the answer to both, *pal*!

⭐ EMLYN'S TEAM ⭐

CHRIS BROAD England's Man of the Series on the glorious tour of 1986/87, scoring centuries in three successive Tests as England retained the Ashes, then won the Perth Cup and the World Series Cup. When not on international duty Chris plays county championship cricket for Nottinghamshire. Emlyn's looking for a good opening innings here.

HANS NIELSEN Latest in the line of great Danish speedway riders. So far has world team, world pairs, and world individual titles to his credit, though what more is there to win? There'll be no problem about speedway questions with Hans, and he claims he's as good at cutting the corners as Emlyn, so Bill's got double trouble in the opposition.

GAME 9
Pictureboard

1

2

3

4

Home & Away

CHRIS
Robinson, Slack, Benson, Athey, and Moxon all opened for England in the 1986 Test series against India and New Zealand, but which man partnered them all?

MO
Goal difference decided the 1985/86 Scottish Championship. Celtic won it, but who were the runners-up?

HANS
America produced a world individual speedway champion in both 1981 and 1982. Name him.

WALTER
On which horse did Lester Piggott win his last Derby?

BILL
Guy Laporte marked his international debut within 60 seconds of the kick-off—but what did he do?

EMLYN
In the 1970s Leeds United had two Scottish international goalkeepers on their books. Name one.

Which British boxer challenged Muhammad Ali for the world heavyweight title in Munich in 1976?

The modern pentathlon includes five disciplines. Riding, fencing, shooting and swimming are the first four, but what comes last?

In which city was cricket last staged as an Olympic sport?

A polo match is divided into 6 periods or 'chukkers', but how long is a chukker?

If the rules require those involved to change lanes each lap, and the man on the inside is responsible for avoiding collisions, what's the sport?

In which sport would you be penalised for going off your 'rocker'?

One-Minute Round

☆ BILL'S TEAM ☆

1 (1 pt) Racing: the Kentucky Derby is staged on which American course?

●

2 (1 pt) Soccer: who scored Scotland's only goal in the 1986 World Cup?

●

3 (1 pt) Tennis: who did Bjorn Borg beat for his first Wimbledon singles title?

●

4 (1 pt) Rugby: which club did Mike Rafter captain to victory in the 1983 John Player Cup?

●

5 (2 pts) Golf: since 1960 only three players have retained the Open title. Name two of them.

●

6 (3 pts) They were winners and champions in 1981—who?
a) World Snooker
b) Davis Cup
c) The Grand National

●

1 (1 pt)   Cricket: in 1986 Gordon Greenidge and Malcolm Marshall topped the batting and bowling averages in the County Championship. Name their county.

2 (1 pt)   Speedway: who partnered Peter Collins to the world pairs title in 1984?

3 (1 pt)   Yachting: which country did *White Crusader* represent in the Americas Cup in Australia?

4 (1 pt)   Soccer: with which club was Kevin Drinkell top scorer when they won promotion to Division One in 1986?

5 (2 pts)   Boxing: which two heavyweights met in 1987 to decide the undisputed championship of the world?

6 (3 pts)   Champions and winners from 1980—name them.
   a) Olympic 1500 m (Men)
   b) Wimbledon Men's Singles
   c) Formula One World Champion

GAME 9
Mystery Personality

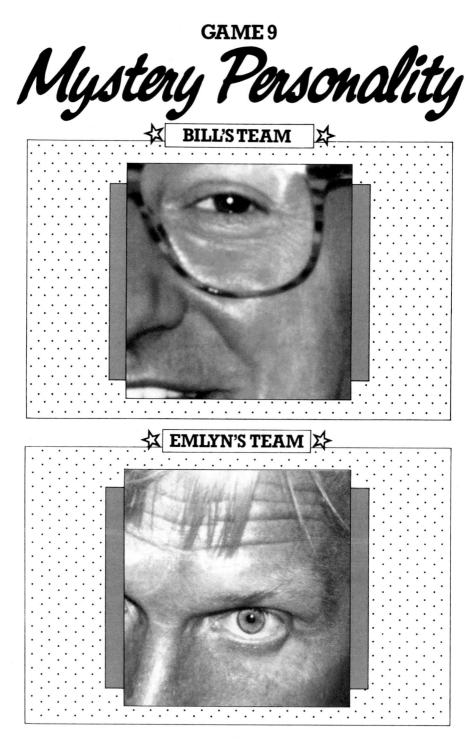

☆ BILL'S TEAM ☆

☆ EMLYN'S TEAM ☆

GAME 9
ANSWERS

PICTUREBOARD

1 Tony Woodcock/Ray Clemence. England striker Tony Woodcock, now playing for Cologne, is trying to beat Spurs goalkeeper Ray Clemence, capped 61 times for England.
2 Steve Cauthen, the first American ever to become champion jockey on the flat in Britain.
3 Michael Holding, who has taken more wickets for the West Indies than any other fast bowler.
4 Eric Gunderson, the former world speedway champion from Sweden.

HOME & AWAY

CHRIS (HOME)
Graham Gooch.

(AWAY)
Richard Dunn. The referee stopped the contest in the fifth round. Five months later Dunn lost his British, Commonwealth and European titles to Joe Bugner, who knocked him out in the first round.

MO (HOME)
Hearts. They needed to beat Dundee to claim the title, but lost 2–0. They were level on points at 50 with Celtic but lost on goal difference.

(AWAY)
Cross-country running.

HANS (HOME)
Bruce Penhall. In 1981 he also took the world pairs title with fellow-American Bobby Schwartz.

(AWAY)
Paris in 1900—Great Britain took the gold, France the silver. It was the only occasion that cricket has been played in the Olympics.

WALTER (HOME)
Teenoso, in 1983—Lester's ninth Derby win since 1954—making him the most successful jockey in the race's history.

(AWAY)
Seven minutes.

BILL (HOME)
He dropped a goal from 50 yards against Ireland in Dublin in 1981. France won 19–13, and went on to the Grand Slam.

(AWAY)
Speed skating. The two competitors swap over at the end of each lap of an oval circuit so that neither has an advantage.

EMLYN (HOME)
David Harvey and David Stewart. Harvey 1965–79 (16 caps). Stewart 1973–78 (1 cap).

(AWAY)
Figure skating. 'Rocker' is one of the compulsory section exercises of the competition.

ONE-MINUTE ROUND

BILL'S TEAM
1 Churchill Downs.
2 Gordon Strachan, scoring in the 2–1 defeat by West Germany in Group E on 8 June 1986 in Queretaro.
3 Ilie Nastase in 1976. Borg won in straight sets 6–4 6–2 9–7.
4 Bristol, beating Leicester 28–22 for their first win.
5 Arnold Palmer 1961/62, Lee Trevino 1971/72, and Tom Watson 1982/83—an all-American trio!
6 a) Steve Davis   b) USA   c) Aldaniti.

EMLYN'S TEAM
1 Hampshire.
2 Chris Morton, his fellow rider at Belle Vue.
3 Great Britain.
4 Norwich City. His tally—22 goals.
5 Mike Tyson and Tony Tucker at the Las Vegas Hilton. Tyson won on a unanimous points decision after 12 rounds.
6 a) Sebastian Coe   b) Bjorn Borg   c) Alan Jones (of Australia).

MYSTERY PERSONALITY

BILL'S TEAM   Dennis Taylor, the world snooker champion in 1985 who comes from Northern Ireland.
EMLYN'S TEAM   Greg Norman, the Australian golfer nicknamed 'the Great White Shark'. Winner of the British Open in 1986.

GAME 10

Snooker, soccer, golf and rugby are highlighted by the guests for Game 10. Emlyn's team includes Jimmy White, who's expected to be as quick with the answers as he is on the snooker table, and Danish international Jan Molby. With Bill are the '87 Open golf champion Nick Faldo and Welsh fly-half Jonathan Davies.

☆ BILL'S TEAM ☆

NICK FALDO The youngest ever English amateur golf champion, who emerged from two lean years to win the biggest prize of all—the Open—in 1987. He'd spent the time remodelling his swing, and it showed! The Ryder Cup star has commented that it's easier to get out of bunkers than it is to get out of answering questions on the programme.

JONATHAN DAVIES Stylish fly-half for Wales, and a member of the side that finished in third place in the '87 World Cup after being beaten by eventual winners New Zealand. Team-mates now call him 'Daffy' after he appeared in a pool with three rubber ducks as a Mystery Personality for *A Question of Sport*. The trouble we get people into! Has suggested to Bill that as an ex-England rugby captain he must find it strange being on the winning side!

☆ EMLYN'S TEAM ☆

JAN MOLBY Since moving from Ajax to Anfield the great Dane has helped Liverpool to their League and FA Cup double of '86, and been christened 'Rambo' by the famous Anfield Kop. Now has a pronounced Scouse accent, and claims to have had no problems with the language—even believes he speaks English better than Ian Rush and Kenny Dalglish. Played for Denmark in the World Cup in Mexico in midfield.

JIMMY WHITE 'The Whirlwind', who first enjoyed success by becoming English amateur champion at sixteen, took just two years to become the youngest ever amateur world champion, and is widely recognised even by his fellow professionals as the most gifted snooker player of them all. Has reached number two in the world—inevitably behind Steve Davis—but is number one for entertainment value.

Pictureboard

1

2

3

4

?

GAME 10

Home & Away

JAN
From which European side did Jesper Olsen sign for Manchester United?

Only one country has appeared in all Winter and Summer Olympic Games since 1896. Name it.

NICK
Who beat Lanny Wadkins at the first play-off hole to win the 1987 US PGA Championship?

What's a toxophilite expected to be good at?

JIMMY
Who scored no less than five televised century breaks in winning the 1986 UK Snooker Championship?

In which sport did Frieda Zamba of the USA win World Championships in 1985, 1986 and 1987?

JONATHAN
Which Welshman, in 1971, set the points scoring record for the British Lions on an overseas tour?

How many periods of play make up an ice hockey match?

EMLYN
Who, in 1983, scored the last penalty to be awarded in an FA Cup Final?

The Pau International, the Kings Cup, the Palamos and the Renns Race are four major events—but what's the sport?

BILL
In 1984, 1985. 1986 and 1987 Bath were winners of the John Player Cup—but which west country club won in 1983?

Which Winter Olympic sport entails a combination of cross-country skiing and shooting?

One-Minute Round

☆ **EMLYN'S TEAM** ☆

1 (1 pt) Soccer: who was the only English referee to officiate in the 1986 World Cup Finals?

2 (1 pt) Snooker: who won the first World Championship to be staged at the Crucible, in Sheffield?

3 (1 pt) Athletics: who was the last Briton to hold the world 5000 m record?

4 (1 pt) Cricket: for which county did Australian skipper Allan Border play in the 1986 County Championship season?

5 (2 pts) Who's the only footballer to have been voted European Player of the Year three years running?

6 (3 pts) By their surnames they could be members of the aristocracy—who are they?

 a) Cricket: Collis (?)

 b) Darts: Stefan (?)

 c) Motor cycling: Geoff (?)

1 (1 pt)   Rugby: for which League side did Robert Ackerman sign when he stopped playing rugby union?

●

2 (1 pt)   Golf: who did Bob Tway beat at the last hole to win the 1986 US PGA title?

●

3 (1 pt)   Name the only Far Eastern country to have staged the Winter Olympics.

●

4 (1 pt)   Which World Championship is contested at Frimley Green?

●

5 (2 pts)   Rugby: for which club does England skipper Mike Harrison play?

●

6 (3 pts)   They are all famous sporting sons from Wales—name them.

a) Boxing: Howard (?)

b) The Marathon: Steve (?)

c) Show jumping: Col. Harry (?)

●

GAME 10
Mystery Personality

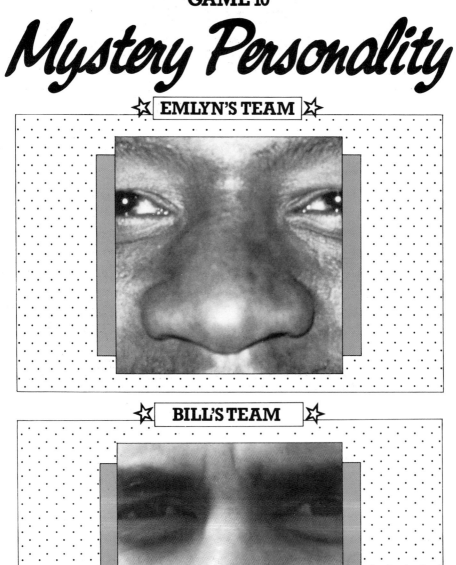

☆ **EMLYN'S TEAM** ☆

☆ **BILL'S TEAM** ☆

GAME 10
ANSWERS

PICTUREBOARD

1 Michael Laudrup, the Danish international footballer who plays for Juventus in the Italian League.
2 Rex Williams, snooker professional. He is chairman of snooker's governing body.
3 Gary Player, the South African golfer who's won every major title, including the Open Championship on both sides of the Atlantic.
4 Ciaran Fitzgerald, the former skipper of the Irish and the British Lions rugby teams.

HOME & AWAY

JAN (HOME)
Ajax of Amsterdam.

(AWAY)
Great Britain.

NICK (HOME)
Larry Nelson, winning with an 8-foot putt on the 19th green to win his second PGA title.

(AWAY)
Archery. 'Toxophily' comes from the Greek word *toxon*, meaning a bow.

JIMMY (HOME)
Steve Davis. He went on to the final where he beat Neal Foulds.

(AWAY)
Surfing.

JONATHAN (HOME)
Barry John, with a total of 188 points on the tour to Australia and New Zealand.

(AWAY)
Three, and they're 20 minutes' duration each.

EMLYN (HOME)
Arnold Muhren for Manchester United in the replay against Brighton—which United won 4-0.

(AWAY)
Pigeon racing.

BILL (HOME)
Bristol, beating Leicester 28–22 in the final.

(AWAY)
The biathlon.

ONE-MINUTE ROUND

EMLYN'S TEAM
1 George Courtney.
2 John Spencer, in 1977. He beat Cliff Thorburn 25–21.
3 David Moorcroft.
4 Essex.
5 Michel Platini of France and Juventus, now retired. He won the award in 1983/84/85.
6 a) Collis King b) Stefan Lord c) Geoff Duke.

BILL'S TEAM
1 Whitehaven.
2 Greg Norman.
3 Japan: Sapporo 1972.
4 World Darts Championships.
5 Wakefield, leading them to the Yorkshire County Championship in 1987.
6 a) Howard Winstone b) Steve Jones c) Col. Harry Llewellyn.

MYSTERY PERSONALITY

EMLYN'S TEAM   Gary Mason, British heavyweight boxing champion.
BILL'S TEAM   Sunil Gavaskar, Indian opening batsman who has scored more Test runs than any other player.

GAME 11

Emlyn's captaincy will be seriously under threat for this one, at least judging by Ian Botham's past appearances. Todd Bennett makes up the trio, whilst Bill's gone for the midfield organising skills of Everton's Peter Reid, and with skier Martin Bell it should be downhill all the way.

✠ BILL'S TEAM ✠

PETER REID The Everton and England international is most definitely the joker in the pack, but a fighter too. He has come back from serious injury several times, and no one would begrudge him the success of League Championship, FA Cup, and European Cup Winners Cup honours he's enjoyed since moving to Goodison. He was voted Players' Player of the Year in 1985 and is still a valued member of the England squad.

MARTIN BELL Britain's number one has been skiing since he was just six years old. Cheerfully admits he's also been falling over on and off ever since! Has now moved up into the world's top twenty skiers and finished a very creditable 16th in the 1987 World Championships. Proved very helpful to Bill on his first appearance on the programme, particularly over pronunciation—although when Bill repeated his words they sounded totally different.

✠ EMLYN'S TEAM ✠

TODD BENNETT Has been one of Britain's best athletes over 400 metres for years. Has a collection of medals from Commonwealth, European, World and Olympic championships both indoor and out. Twice European indoor champion, and a member of the Great Britain relay squad who took the silver in the Los Angeles Olympics.

IAN BOTHAM Unquestionably the world's greatest all-rounder in cricket. Has taken more Test wickets than any other player in history, and scored over 5000 Test runs. Just about won the Ashes for England in 1981 single-handed, and since his Test debut has only ever been dropped for disciplinary reasons. Played League soccer for Scunthorpe—though not as well as he has played county cricket for Somerset, and latterly Worcestershire. Leukaemia research collected a million pounds when he walked the length of the country.

GAME 11
Pictureboard

1

2

3

4

?

GAME 11

Home & Away

PETER
Merseyside finished one and two in the 1986/87 season—but which club was third?

Motor racing: where did Nigel Mansell race his 100th Grand Prix?

TODD
Who, in 1976, completed an Olympic double in the men's 400 and 800 m finals?

In which sport do you encounter a blue line?

MARTIN
Which Swedish skier completed a hat-trick of slalom world titles between 1978 and 1982?

Soutomaior has already won two World Formula One Championship titles—by what name is he better known?

IAN
Which overseas player did the double of 100 wickets and 1000 runs in a County Championship season in 1984?

What sport requires you to throw stones at houses?

BILL
Which country ended up waiting until 1968 to record its first Grand Slam?

If you were reading the 'Telegraph' on the fifth, what would you be about to do?

EMLYN
Which club set the record of 11 straight wins in opening a First Division Championship season?

If you pot a pink with every red in a complete clearance of a snooker table what would be your score?

GAME 11
One-Minute Round

1 (1 pt)   Rugby union: which English player between 1955 and 1962 set the record for the number of appearances for the British Lions?

●

2 (1 pt)   Soccer: which club did Chris Woods leave to join Rangers?

●

3 (1 pt)   Motor cycling: which track staged the 1987 British Grand Prix?

●

4 (1 pt)   Skiing: who was overall world champion for three years running?

●

5 (2 pts)   Golf: who were the beaten semi-finalists in the 1987 Dunhill Cup?

●

6 (3 pts)   They were all winners and champions in 1980—name them:

a) National Hunt Champion Jockey

b) Soccer: European Cup

c) Cricket: County Champions

●

1 (1 pt) Soccer: Di Stefano was capped by three countries. Spain and Colombia were two—name the third.

2 (1 pt) Cricket: which country had a shock win over Australia in the opening match of the 1983 World Cup?

3 (1 pt) Yachting: what is the final race in the Admiral's Cup series?

4 (1 pt) Racing: name the only horse to have won the Championship Chase three times at the National Hunt Festival.

5 (2 pts) Squash: which two ladies contested the 1987 World Championship?

6 (3 pts) Yellow and red are two of the five coloured rings on the Olympic flag—name the other three.

GAME 11
Mystery Personality

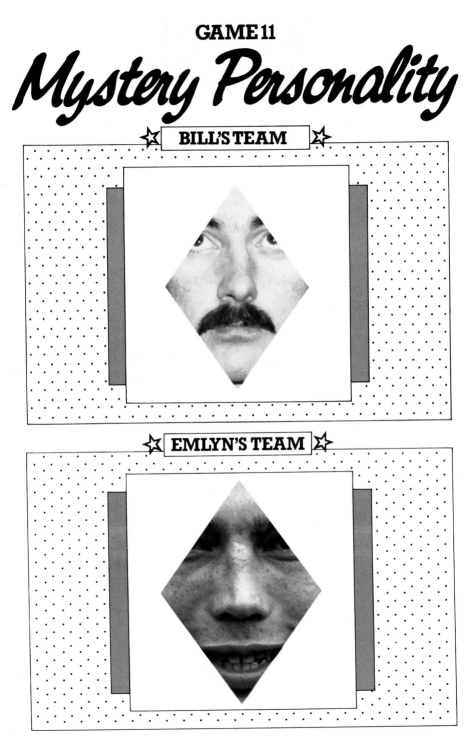

☆ **BILL'S TEAM** ☆

☆ **EMLYN'S TEAM** ☆

GAME 11 ANSWERS

PICTUREBOARD

1 Bruce Grobbelaar, the Liverpool goalkeeper.
2 Bill Johnson, the first American skier to win an Olympic gold medal in the men's downhill, which he did in 1984.
3 Phil Brown, a member of the British 400 m relay team that finished second in the 1987 World Championships.
4 Graham Dilley, the England and Worcestershire fast bowler.

HOME & AWAY

PETER (HOME)
Tottenham. Everton took the title with Liverpool runners-up.

(AWAY)
Austria in 1987. It was the same track on which he began his F1 career. He won then, too.

TODD (HOME)
Alberto Juantorena of Cuba. Though favourite at 400 m, he was unknown at 800 m. He won that in world record time! In all he ran nine races, losing 11 lb in weight.

(AWAY)
Ice hockey. The blue lines divide the playing surface into three zones.

MARTIN (HOME)
Ingemar Stenmark, winning in 1978, 1980 and 1982, and also winning the Giant Slalom title in 1978 and 1982.

(AWAY)
Nelson Piquet, world champion in 1981 and 1983.

IAN (HOME)
Richard Hadlee of Nottinghamshire, though the county had to settle for second place behind Essex, despite Hadlee's efforts.

(AWAY)
Curling. The curling 'stones' are delivered to the target—or 'tee'—which is in the centre of the 'house' at the end of the rink.

BILL (HOME)
France. It took them 39 years of competition to win, having joined the Championship in 1910 and suffered several breaks in participation over the years.

(AWAY)
Putting. The Telegraph is the fifth hole on the Royal Liverpool course at Hoylake.

EMLYN (HOME)
Tottenham, in the 1960/61 season, when they finished champions with 31 wins out of 42 games.

(AWAY)
132: 15 reds (15 pts), 15 pinks (90 pts) and 27 pts for the colours.

ONE-MINUTE ROUND

BILL'S TEAM
1 Dickie Jeeps, with 13 appearances. (Ireland's Willie John McBride went on to make 17 appearances before retiring.)
2 Norwich City, for whom he made 206 appearances between 1979 and 1986.
3 Donington Park.
4 Phil Mahre (USA), breaking a European domination going back to the 1960s and Jean-Claude Killy.
5 The holders: Australia and the USA.
6 a) Jonjo O'Neill, for the second time. b) Notts Forest, for the second year. c) Middlesex—their eighth championship title.

EMLYN'S TEAM
1 Argentina, his country by birth. He moved from there to Colombia, then on to Spain to play for Real Madrid, eventually taking Spanish nationality.
2 Zimbabwe. It was their only win in the competition, which was eventually won by India.
3 The Fastnet Race from the Solent to the Fastnet lighthouse off the southern tip of Ireland, and back to Plymouth.
4 Badsworth Boy. A unique feat for a horse that as a 2-year old was raced on the flat by Willie Carson!
5 Susan Devoy of New Zealand and Britain's Lisa Opie. It was staged in Auckland, New Zealand. Devoy won 9–3; 10–8; 9–2; retaining the title.
6 Blue, green and black, each of the rings signifying one of the five continents of the world.

MYSTERY PERSONALITY

BILL'S TEAM   Willie Miller, international footballer, captain of Aberdeen. He has earned over 50 caps for Scotland.
EMLYN'S TEAM   Rory Underwood, the English rugby union back who is a fighter pilot in the RAF.

GAME 12

Stars come and go, but their achievements live on long after. Bionic Barry Sheene and Steve Smith, Bill's successor as captain of the England side, join Emlyn for this game, whilst Olympic gold medallist Lynn Davies will be propping up Bill with *enfant terrible* and soccer genius George Best.

☆ BILL'S TEAM ☆

GEORGE BEST Left Belfast to join Manchester United, and proceeded to become a footballing legend. Won two Championship medals with the club, as well as a European Cup winners' medal, and in the same year—1968—was Footballer of the Year both here and in Europe. Won 37 caps for Northern Ireland, and his fame was worldwide. He appeared on the first ever *Question of Sport* programme on Monday 5 January 1970.

LYNN DAVIES The Welsh love their heroes, and Lynn certainly became one when he won the Olympic long jump gold medal in 1964 in Tokyo. He went on to become both Commonwealth and European champion, and dominated the long jump event at that time. He was also a fine sprinter in his day, though he did have to settle for second place behind George Best. Why? Well, he was a guest on the second showing of *Question of Sport*!

☆ EMLYN'S TEAM ☆

BARRY SHEENE Almost as well-known as the picture of his legs pinned back together again after his 1975 crash at Daytona! Despite many injuries Barry made it to world motor-cycling champion in both 1976 and 1977. Retired to take up the less dangerous sport of truck-racing. One of Britain's most popular sports stars ever.

STEVE SMITH 'Smithy' is one of sport's great characters, with a renowned sense of humour. Was scrum-half in the England side skippered to the Grand Slam by Bill in 1980, and went on to take over as captain when Bill retired. Won 28 caps in all, and was flown out to New Zealand in 1983 as an emergency replacement for the British Lions. In the first game he played he was appointed captain!

Pictureboard

1

2

3

4

?

GAME 12
Home & Away

BARRY
Who was the legendary Italian rider who won no less than 15 world titles at 350 and 500 cc?

Indulgence, Juno and Jamarella were Great Britain's representatives in 1987. What was the event?

GEORGE
Manchester United were the first British club to spend a six-figure transfer fee—from which Italian club did they sign Denis Law?

A Touch of Class was worth gold at the Los Angeles Olympics, and Joe Fargis collected it. Name the sport.

STEVE
Which city staged the inaugural World Cup Final?

If you had collected the Grand Challenge Cup, or the Silver Goblets, or the Princess Elizabeth Cup, where would you be competing?

LYNN
In the 1960 Rome Olympics Ralph Boston's gold medal leap of 26 ft 7¾ ins beat the record set 24 years earlier—by whom?

Against which country do the West Indies play their Test matches for the Frank Worrell Trophy?

EMLYN
Name the only London club never to have played in the First Division.

Which famous English sporting venue staged the Australian Rules match between Carlton and North Melbourne?

BILL
Which side defeated Taraniki to win the 1987 Ranfurly Shield?

In which sport are you awarded three points for a 'Sliothar' under the bar, and only one point for getting over it?

☆ **EMLYN'S TEAM** ☆

1 (1 pt)   Motor cycling: which American in 1985 became the first rider to hold world titles simultaneously at 250 and 500 cc levels?

2 (1 pt)   Rugby: which club side plays at Kingsholm?

3 (1 pt)   Soccer: who captained Italy to World Cup success in 1982?

4 (1 pt)   Golf: in which year did Gary Player win the first of his three Open titles?

5 (2 pts)   Which two countries met in the men's Olympic Hockey final in Los Angeles in 1984?

6 (3 pts)   With what sports do you associate the following terms?
   a) Dormie (?)
   b) Slap-shot (?)
   c) Boast (?)

1 (1 pt) Soccer: who is Northern Ireland's most-capped player?

2 (1 pt) Athletics: who won the men's long jump at the 1983 World Championships in Helsinki?

3 (1 pt) Racing: on which horse did Hywel Davies win the 1985 Grand National?

4 (1 pt) Rugby: when was the four-point try introduced?

5 (2 pts) Cricket: who were the captains when the MCC played the Rest of the World to celebrate the MCC's Bicentenary at Lord's?

6 (3 pts) These three world professional boxing champions also won Olympic gold medals—but at which Games?

    a) Michael Spinks (?)

    b) Muhammad Ali (?)

    c) Floyd Patterson (?)

GAME 12
Mystery Personality

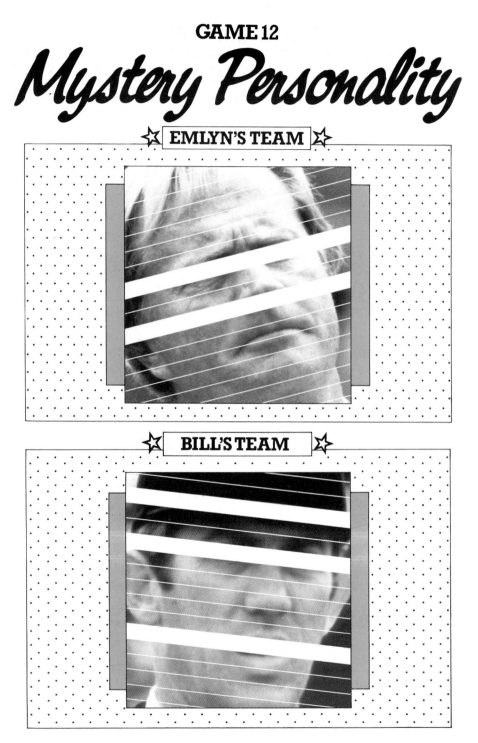

☆ EMLYN'S TEAM ☆

☆ BILL'S TEAM ☆

GAME 12
ANSWERS

PICTUREBOARD

1 Colin Deans, who played for Hawick, Scotland and the British Lions.
2 Kenny Dalglish, of Liverpool and Scotland. Most capped Scottish footballer.
3 Bob Beamon, the American long jumper who shattered the world record in the 1968 Olympics.
4 Jack Brabham, the Australian motor racing driver. World champion on three occasions.

HOME & AWAY

BARRY (HOME)
Giacomo Agostini. Between 1968 and 1972 he was world champion at both, but also won a further two world titles at 350 cc and three at 500 cc.

(AWAY)
The Admiral's Cup, in which the British team finished second behind New Zealand.

GEORGE (HOME)
Torino, in July 1962, paying £115,000 to bring Law back to English football.

(AWAY)
Show-jumping. Joe won two gold medals—both individual and team—with the USA.

STEVE (HOME)
Auckland, New Zealand. New Zealand beat France in the final, and stayed undefeated in the tournament.

(AWAY)
Henley Regatta. They are various prizes to be won for rowing. The Silver Goblets is perhaps the most famous.

LYNN (HOME)
Jesse Owens. The legendary American athlete leapt 26 ft 5½ ins in Berlin, where he won four gold medals in all.

(AWAY)
Australia.

EMLYN (HOME)
Millwall.

(AWAY)
The Oval on 11 October 1987.

BILL (HOME)   (AWAY)
Auckland by the overwhelming   Hurling.
total of 46–6 at Eden Park.

ONE-MINUTE ROUND

EMLYN'S TEAM
1 Freddie Spencer.
2 Gloucester.
3 Dino Zoff.
4 1959. He also won in 1968 and 1974.
5 West Germany and Pakistan. Pakistan won 2–1 and England collected bronze.
6 a) Golf (i.e. a player 3 up with 3 holes to play is lying dormie)   b) Ice hockey.   c) Squash.

BILL'S TEAM
1 Pat Jennings, with 110 appearances.
2 Carl Lewis. The American also won the 100 m.
3 Last Suspect.
4 1972, the same year in which Scotland and Wales refused to play in Dublin because of increased violence in Northern Ireland.
5 Mike Gatting for the MCC and Allan Border for the Rest of the World.
6 a) 1976 Montreal.   b) 1960 Rome.   c) 1952 Helsinki.

MYSTERY PERSONALITY

EMLYN'S TEAM   Jack Nicklaus, the American golfer known as the 'Golden Bear'. Winner of every major tournament in the world and British Open Champion three times.
BILL'S TEAM   David Broome, still one of Great Britain's leading show jumpers and an Olympic medallist.

GAME 13

Athletics, soccer, swimming and rugby union form the basis of this Game 13—and the Dutch influence is much in evidence with Nelli Cooman despite the fact she's only 5 ft 1½ ins tall. She's on Bill's team, along with Tony Cottee, while Emlyn has swimmer Adrian Moorhouse, and rugby's John Jeffrey.

⭐ BILL'S TEAM ⭐

TONY COTTEE Unique for keeping a record of each and every match in which he plays, the England Under-21 and England squad member won the accolade of his fellow professionals when he was voted Young Player of the Year in 1986. So far he has remained a one-club man, having joined West Ham as an apprentice in September 1982—and scoring for them on his first team debut.

NELLI COOMAN Born in Surinam, the little Dutch girl has already won indoor athletic titles over 60 m at the European and World Championships, setting the world record in the process. She was a bronze medallist at the European Championships in Stuttgart over 100 m. Her English is as good as Bill's, though she's a bit short on knowledge of his sport, rugby union. However, she's bound to be quick off the mark on the athletics stuff!

⭐ EMLYN'S TEAM ⭐

ADRIAN MOORHOUSE The first man in the world to swim the 100 m short course in under a minute, and—with a dozen medals in all—the possessor of an enviable number of medals at Commonwealth and European level, though he's yet to collect Olympic or world honours. His speed through the water is matched only by his speed on his home questions: if Emlyn needs anyone to help him stay afloat against Bill then Adrian's the man.

JOHN JEFFREY The Kelso loose forward first gained international recognition when picked for Scotland to play Australia in 1984. Now established in the side, and a member of the World Cup squad 'down under' in Australia and New Zealand, he has won a reputation for skill both in defence and attack—just what Emlyn needs.

Pictureboard

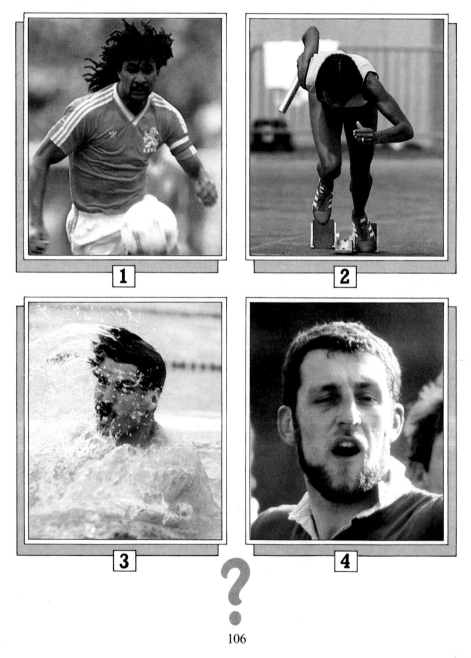

1

2

3

4

?

Home & Away

TONY
Who did Spurs beat in the all-London FA Cup Final of 1982?

ADRIAN
Which American swimmer won 100 m and 200 m breaststroke medals at both the 1972 and 1976 Olympic Games?

NELLI
Can you name either of the American girls who finished first and second in the women's 200 m final in the Los Angeles Olympic Games?

JOHN
Scotland's John Rutherford and Roy Laidlaw hold the world record for a half-back partnership, but which Welsh pairing previously held it?

BILL
In which country is the Currie Cup contested?

EMLYN
If you were watching Be Quick against Go Ahead in which European country would you be?

In which sport would you find 'hashmarks' on the field of play?

Which sport forbids any competitors to play left-handed?

On the field of play you'd find 12 pieces of wood, and under given circumstances an absolute maximum of 15 players. What's the sport?

If you were overcoming a Hog's Back, Brush and Rails, and a Double Oxer, what would you be doing?

In cycling, who traditionally wears a white jersey with red polka dots?

Which American football side plays at Candlestick Park?

One-Minute Round

☆ BILL'S TEAM ☆

1 (1 pt)   Rugby: when did Wales make their first short tour of Australia?

2 (1 pt)   Athletics: which city hosted the last World Athletics Championships?

3 (1 pt)   Tennis: who was the last British girl to win the US Open title?

4 (1 pt)   Soccer: where did Brazil win its last World Cup?

5 (2 pts)   At which event did Great Britain's Kathy Tayler and Wendy Norman become world champions?

6 (3 pts)   You could find their surnames in a courtroom—can you complete them?

a) Soccer: Alan (?)

b) Tennis: Jo (?)

c) Speedway: Simon (?)

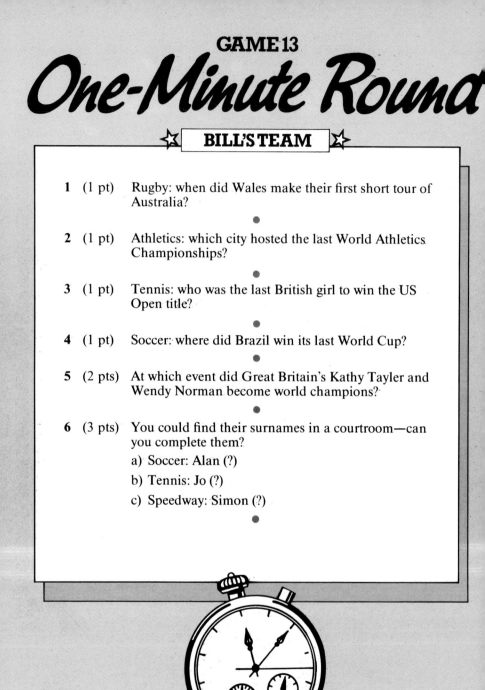

1 (1 pt) Soccer: which Portuguese side did Tommy Docherty manage?

2 (1 pt) Rugby: for which side did Bill Beaumont play his club rugby?

3 (1 pt) Motor racing: name the last Australian to be World Formula One Champion.

4 (1 pt) Swimming: in which event did Steve Lundquist set a world record in the 1984 Olympics?

5 (2 pts) Which sport staged its World Open Championships at Birmingham's National Exhibition Centre in the summer of 1987?

6 (3 pts) Their surnames might also be found in a quarry—who are they?
a) High jump: Dwight (?)
b) Rugby: Ray (?)
c) Soccer: Bob (?)

GAME 13
Mystery Personality

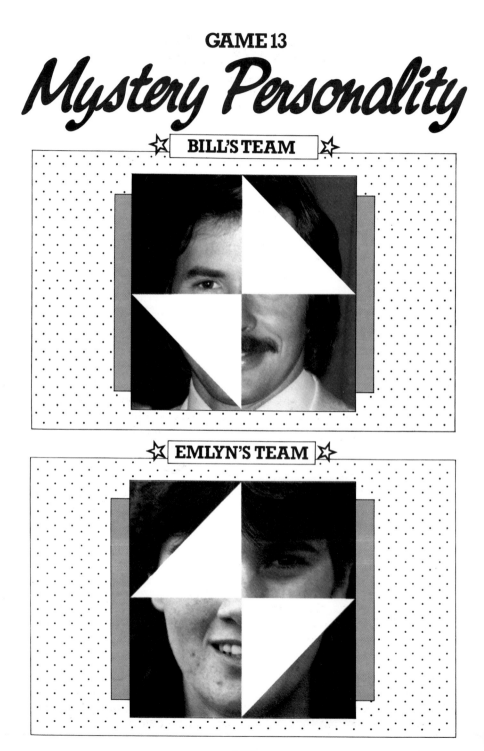

☆ **BILL'S TEAM** ☆

☆ **EMLYN'S TEAM** ☆

GAME 13
ANSWERS

PICTUREBOARD

1 Ruud Gullit, the Dutch footballer now playing with AC Milan.
2 Evelyn Ashford, the Olympic 100 m champion from Los Angeles.
3 Mark Spitz, the American swimmer who won seven gold medals at the 1972 Montreal Olympics.
4 Wade Dooley. From modest beginnings with Preston Grasshoppers this giant forward gained international recognition with his first cap for England in 1985. Now playing his club rugby on Bill's old stamping ground in Fylde.

HOME & AWAY

TONY (HOME)
Queen's Park Rangers, in a match which went to a replay and was decided 1–0 through a Glen Hoddle penalty.

(AWAY)
American grid-iron football. They are marked between each field stripe and used by match officials to place accurately the ball for resumption of play.

ADRIAN (HOME)
John Henken. He took 100 m bronze and 200 m gold in Munich in 1972, and the 100 m gold and 200 m silver in Montreal in 1976. Both gold-winning performances were in new world record times.

(AWAY)
Polo, to prevent nasty accidents between the riders during play.

NELLI (HOME)
Valerie Brisco-Hooks (NWR) and Florence Griffith. Merlene Ottey-Page of Jamaica was third.

(AWAY)
Cricket. There are 11 fielders, two batsmen, two runners, six stumps and four bails! Plus two bats of course.

JOHN (HOME)
Phil Bennett and Gareth Edwards. who were partners in 29 International Board matches.

(AWAY)
Riding. They are types of obstacle to be found in a jumping ring, or on a cross-country course.

BILL (HOME)
South Africa. The cup is played for by regional teams annually.

(AWAY)
The King of the Mountains (the winner of the most mountain stages)—mainly during the Tour de France.

EMLYN (HOME)
Holland. Be Quick Groningen and Go Ahead Deventer are both former Dutch League Championship winners.

(AWAY)
The San Francisco 49ers.

ONE-MINUTE ROUND

BILL'S TEAM
1 1978. Surprisingly, they lost both Test matches under Terry Cobner's captaincy.
2 Rome—1987.
3 Virginia Wade. In 1968, beating Billie Jean King 6–4 6–2 in the final.
4 Mexico, in 1970, beating Italy 4–1 in the final.
5 Modern Pentathlon: Kathy Tayler in 1979, and Wendy Norman in 1980 and 1982.
6 a) Alan Judge   b) Jo Durie   c) Simon Wigg.

EMLYN'S TEAM
1 Oporto.
2 Fylde.
3 Alan Jones, in 1980 in a Williams-Ford.
4 The men's 100 m breaststroke in a time of 1 minute 01.65 seconds.
5 Squash.
6 a) Dwight Stones   b) Ray Gravell   c) Bob Bolder.

MYSTERY PERSONALITY

BILL'S TEAM   David Wilkie, gold medallist in the 200 m breaststroke at the 1973 World Championships, the 1974 Commonwealth Games and the 1976 Olympics.
EMLYN'S TEAM   Kathy Cook, recently retired track athlete. Her distinguished career included Commonwealth Games and World Championship medals, and she represented Great Britain in the 1980 Olympics.

GAME 14

For this game Emlyn has enlisted the help of Allan Lamb, the England batsman, and being a rugby league fan himself, he couldn't resist recruiting Kiwi Test centre Mark Elia as well. Bill has Spurs striker Clive Allen and Welsh athlete Kirsty Wade joining him.

☆ BILL'S TEAM ☆

CLIVE ALLEN The top-scoring Spurs forward and England international who became Player of the Year in 1987, and despite the arguments, overtook Jimmy Greaves's seemingly unbeaten scoring record. He's still remembered for being the centre of that £1-million merry-go-round in 1980 when he moved from Queen's Park Rangers to Arsenal and on to Crystal Palace without kicking a ball. Looks to have the scoring record that Bill needs.

KIRSTY WADE Became the first Welsh girl to win a Commonwealth Games gold medal back in 1982, over 800 m, and repeated that in 1986 in Edinburgh. She later became the fastest ever British girl over 800 m, and has set Commonwealth records at both the mile and 1000 m indoors. Has recently switched to the 1500 m, reaching the final of the World Championships in Rome in 1987.

☆ EMLYN'S TEAM ☆

MARK ELIA Te Atatu—not a foreign swear word, but the Auckland club for which Elia plays back home in New Zealand. He was the Kiwis' top scoring centre when they toured Great Britain in 1985, and subsequently played for St Helens, making the Challenge Cup final in 1987. Despite scoring once, and having two tries disallowed, he ended up with a loser's medal but doesn't plan on the same thing happening to him or Emlyn.

ALLAN LAMB The South-African born batsman plays his county cricket for Northants, and his international cricket for England. He was a member of the tour party which swept the honours board in Australia in 1986/87 Since his Test debut in 1982 he has made nearly 60 appearances in the England side, and was a member of the World Cup squad which played in India and Pakistan in 1987.

113

Pictureboard

GAME 14
Home & Away

MARK
In the third and final Test between Great Britain and New Zealand in 1985, all Britain's points in the 6–all draw came from penalties kicked by the player who came on as sub. Name him.

Where would you find Redgate Corner?

CLIVE
Who appeared for Brighton in the 1983 FA Cup, for Liverpool in the 1984 League Cup, and for Queen's Park Rangers in the League Cup in 1985: three Finals, three years, three clubs?

Who is Britain's most successful driver in the Le Mans 24-hr race?

ALLAN
Which Lancashire club did Viv Richards join after leaving Somerset?

How many innings per side would you find in a game of baseball?

KIRSTY
Which American set a world record for the women's mile of 4:16.71 in Zurich in August 1985?

In which sport might the winner need to use no flickers at all, whilst those behind him several?

EMLYN
Soccer: which country won Olympic gold in Los Angeles in 1984?

In which sport might you round off with a 'roundoff'?

BILL
Who was the last Scotsman to captain the British Lions?

Wembley Stadium was the scene for the inaugural World Championships in which sport in 1936? Its winners include Lionel Van Praag, Peter Craven, Jerzy Szczakiel.

One-Minute Round

☆ EMLYN'S TEAM ☆

1 (1 pt) Soccer: who scored the opening goal in the all-Merseyside FA Cup Final of 1986?

2 (1 pt) Rugby league: who did Warrington beat for the Premiership Trophy in 1986?

3 (1 pt) Athletics: at which event did Jon Ridgeon win a silver medal in the 1987 World Championships in Rome?

4 (1 pt) Cricket: Neil Foster was the only Englishman to take more than 100 first class wickets in the summer of 1986—for which county?

5 (2 pts) Hockey: which two countries contested the 1987 World Championship Final?

6 (3 pts) Their surnames are items you'd find in the larder:
a) Tennis: David (?)
b) Athletics: Gary (?)
c) Racing: Martin (?)

1 (1 pt) Rugby union: which Scottish club plays at Poynder Park?

●

2 (1 pt) Athletics: who was the only British girl to reach the women's 800 m Olympic final in Los Angeles?

●

3 (1 pt) Soccer: which club, then in the Second Division, won the FA Cup in 1980?

●

4 (1 pt) Skating: at which Olympic Games did John Curry win gold in the figure skating competition?

●

5 (2 pts) Show-jumping: John and Michael Whittaker apart, name the other two riders who made up the British team which won the European team title in the 1987 championships in Switzerland.

●

6 (3 pts) You might find their surnames on a bush—complete them:

a) Swimming: Murray (?)

b) Soccer: George (?)

c) Snooker: Willie (?)

●

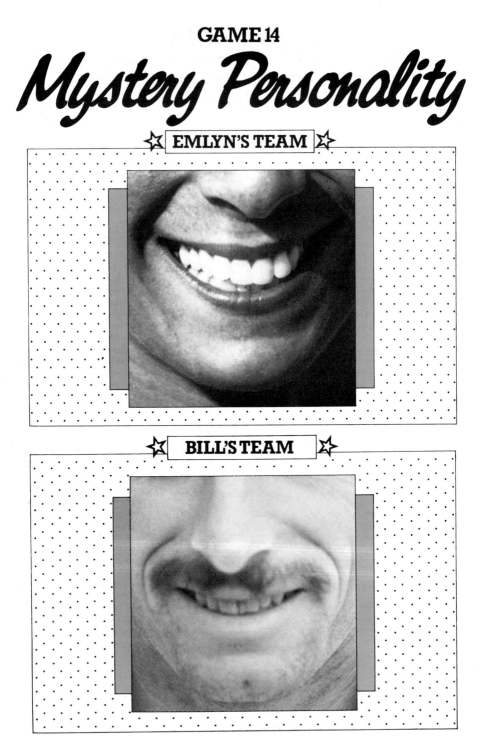

GAME 14
Mystery Personality

☆ **EMLYN'S TEAM** ☆

☆ **BILL'S TEAM** ☆

118

GAME 14 ANSWERS

PICTUREBOARD

1 Ellery Hanley, captain of the British rugby league team.
2 David Gower, the Leicestershire cricket team captain and a former captain of England.
3 John Barnes, England and Liverpool footballer.
4 Mary Decker-Slaney, American women's distance runner, former world record holder at 5000 m.

HOME & AWAY

MARK (HOME)
Lee Crooks. New Zealand had won the first Test, Great Britain the second. Crooks came on for the injured Andy Goodway 23 minutes in—and kicked three penalties for the draw.

(AWAY)
Donington Park, the setting for the 1987 British Motor Cycling Grand Prix.

CLIVE (HOME)
Michael Robinson. Now playing in Spanish league for Ossasuna.

(AWAY)
Derek Bell has won it four times—three with Jackie Ickx, once with Hans Stuck.

ALLAN (HOME)
Rishton.

(AWAY)
Nine innings per side which equals a total of 18 innings.

KIRSTY (HOME)
Mary Decker-Slaney. Maricica Puica of Rumania set a European best in second place, with Zola Budd third in a Commonwealth and UK best time.

(AWAY)
Speedway. Flickers are clear pieces of perspex which riders tear off after each lap to give them clear vision—hence the leader might not need to use them!

EMLYN (HOME)
France. They beat Brazil 2–0 in the Final.

(AWAY)
Gymnastics. It's a popular move used to complete a tumbling exercise.

BILL (HOME)
Mike Campbell-Lamerton.

(AWAY)
World speedway championships. Lionel Van Praag: winner 1936. Peter Craven: winner 1955 and 1962. Jerzy Szczakiel: winner 1973.

ONE-MINUTE ROUND

EMLYN'S TEAM
1 Gary Lineker for Everton—though they lost 3–1 to Liverpool.
2 Halifax, winning 38–10.
3 The men's 110 m hurdles.
4 Essex.
5 Holland and England. Holland won in a penalty shoot-out after extra time.
6 a) David Mustard   b) Gary Honey   c) Martin Pepper.

BILL'S TEAM
1 Kelso.
2 Lorraine Baker, who finished fifth behind gold medallist Doina Melinte of Rumania.
3 West Ham United, beating Arsenal 1–0 through a goal from Trevor Brooking.
4 1976, at Innsbruck, Austria.
5 Nick Skelton and Malcolm Pyrah.
6 a) Murray Rose   b) George Berry   c) Willie Thorne.

MYSTERY PERSONALITY

EMLYN'S TEAM   Fatima Whitbread, women's javelin world champion in 1987 and past world record holder.
BILL'S TEAM   Richard Hadlee, the New Zealand cricketer chasing Ian Botham's record of 382 Test wickets. He was the last player to do the 'double' of 100 wickets and 1000 runs in an English season.

GAME 15

For all American football fans, Walter Payton, the Chicago Bears running back, has flown over to join Bill's team, where he joins Czech tennis star Helena Sukova. Emlyn sticks to home-grown stuff—but what talent. Ryder Cup star Howard Clark, and 'Superman' Daley Thompson are with him.

⭐ BILL'S TEAM ⭐

WALTER PAYTON The holder of numerous individual NFL records, including all-time marks for touchdowns and 'rushing', he played a major part in the Chicago Bears Superbowl victory of 1986, and has been at the top for 13 seasons. Not bad for a player considered small by grid-iron standards—5 ft 11 ins and 202 lb. His nickname is 'Sweetness'—wonder what Emlyn is going to make of that?

HELENA SUKOVA Her whole family is tennis mad. Dad's president of the Czech Tennis Federation, her late mother appeared in the 1962 Wimbledon ladies singles final, and her brother is on the satellite circuit! She has beaten the mighty Martina, been US Indoor Champion, and is with Claudia Kohde-Kilsch the world's number two doubles pairing. Has been warned by Hana Mandlikova about Emlyn's inability to keep his hands to himself.

⭐ EMLYN'S TEAM ⭐

HOWARD CLARK A professional for fifteen years, he had earned a place in golfing history having been a member of the European team which won back the Ryder Cup in 1985, and then became the first team to win against the Americans on their own ground in 1987 at Muirfield Village, Ohio. Amongst the top money earners on the European circuit, he has three Madrid Open titles to his credit amongst other championships. Knows more than he lets on to!

DALEY THOMPSON How he ever earned the nickname 'Superman' is hard to imagine. He may have dominated the world of the decathlon for the last ten years, become European, World and Olympic champion, world points record holder, and so on . . . but with application and dedication we could all do that, couldn't we? His knowledge of sport is reckoned to be enough to set a world record too. Go to it Daley!

GAME 15
Pictureboard

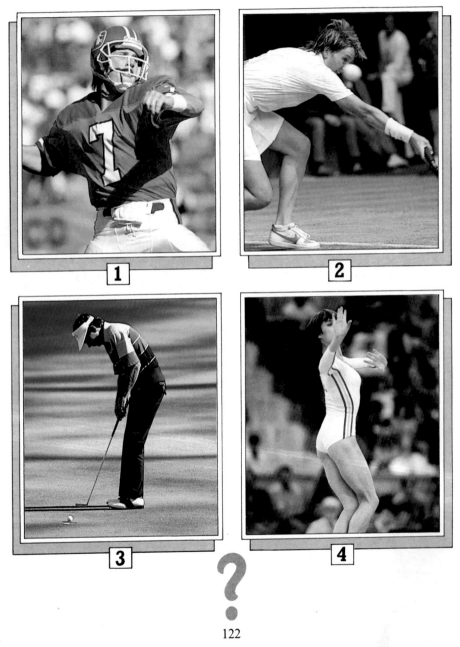

1

2

3

4

?

GAME 15

Home & Away

WALTER
Which American city, famed for its production of steel, also produced a football side which won the Superbowl on all four appearances in 1975, 1976, 1979, and 1980?

In which sport is one always red; two always blue; three white; four black; five orange; and six black and white stripes?

HOWARD
During the 1987 Dunhill Cup at St Andrew's, a new record was set on the old course. Name the player.

With which sport do you connect the terms: Canadian, Heinz, Goliath?

HELENA
Who partnered Martina Navratilova to a grand slam of ladies doubles titles in 1984?

In which English county would you find Belle Vue, Crown Flatt, Wiggington Road, and Fartown?

DALEY
Which American athlete finished tenth in Munich, then became Olympic decathlon champion in Montreal in 1976?

In which sport do the players rotate clockwise one place before service so that each player takes a turn in each position during a set?

BILL
Rugby: which famous Edinburgh Wanderers player captained Wales to the Triple Crown in both 1950 and 1952?

In 1986 this sport held its world championships in a hotel in Bavaria, and in 1988 they'll be held on a ferry boat on the Baltic. What's the sport?

EMLYN
Against which side did the Brazilian Mirandinha score his first goal in British football?

Which famous horse race is nicknamed 'Run for the Roses'?

One-Minute Round

☆ BILL'S TEAM ☆

1 (1 pt)   Rugby: which side traditionally plays the East Midlands for the Mobbs Memorial Trophy?

2 (1 pt)   Baseball: with which side did the legendary Babe Ruth end his career?

3 (1 pt)   Tennis: who partnered Chris Evert to the 1976 Wimbledon ladies doubles title?

4 (1 pt)   Which major championship was staged at the Olympic Club of San Francisco in 1987?

5 (2 pts)   Soccer: which clubs finished second and third behind Everton in the 1986/87 season? A point for each.

6 (3 pts)   Big winners in their year—but who are they?
   a) 1984 Superbowl (?)
   b) 1969 Open Golf (?)
   c) 1975 Men's singles at Wimbledon (?)

1 (1 pt)   Soccer: which nation became the first ever Olympic soccer champions?

2 (1 pt)   Golf: who was runner-up when Greg Norman took the 1986 British Open title?

3 (1 pt)   Athletics: who was Great Britain's only gold medallist in the 1987 world championships in Rome?

4 (1 pt)   Cricket: who replaced Ian Botham in the MCC team for the Bicentennial match at Lord's in 1987?

5 (2 pts)   Tennis: name the winners of the 1987 Wimbledon men's doubles.

6 (3 pts)   Who were winners in these events in these years?
a) 1980 Grand National (?)
b) 1976 FA Cup (?)
c) 1980 Wimbledon ladies singles (?)

GAME 15
Mystery Personality

☆ **BILL'S TEAM** ☆

☆ **EMLYN'S TEAM** ☆

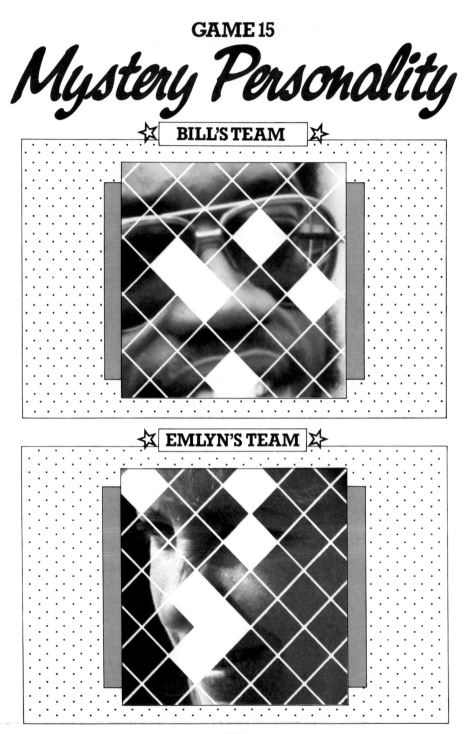

GAME 15
ANSWERS

PICTUREBOARD

1 John Elway, American footballer. He plays quarter back for the Denver Broncos.
2 Anne Hobbs, Britain's number one ladies tennis player.
3 Larry Mize, the American golfer who won the 1987 US Masters.
4 Nadia Comaneci, the Romanian gymnast who won three gold medals and was the star of the 1976 Olympics. She was the first gymnast to score the 'perfect 10'.

HOME & AWAY

WALTER (HOME)
Pittsburgh. The Pittsburgh Steelers won on each and every one of their four Superbowl appearances.

(AWAY)
Greyhound racing. They're the jacket colours for the dogs counting from the inside lanes of the track to the outside—the order of the colours never varies.

HOWARD (HOME)
Rodger Davis (Australia): 62.

(AWAY)
Horse racing. They are all betting terms.

HELENA (HOME)
Pam Shriver.

(AWAY)
Yorkshire. They're all Rugby League club grounds: Wakefield Trinity, Dewsbury, York, and Fartown in that order.

DALEY (HOME)
Bruce Jenner. Jenner's victory was assured after 8 of the 10 events.

(AWAY)
Volleyball.

BILL (HOME)
John Gwilliam.

(AWAY)
World indoor golf championships. The 1986 championship in the Bavarian Alps hotel was won by the Finns—hence the fact that Finland will host the next. Stormy weather could add a new meaning to the term 'water hazard'.

EMLYN (HOME)
The Irish League, playing for the Football League in a friendly at Windsor Park, Belfast in September 1987. The final score was 2–2.

(AWAY)
The Kentucky Derby. The winner receives a garland of roses in the shape of a horseshoe.

ONE-MINUTE ROUND

BILL'S TEAM
1 The Barbarians.
2 New York Yankees.
3 Martina Navratilova. They beat Billie Jean King and Betty Stove 6–1 3–6 7–5.
4 The US Open Golf Championship, won by outsider Scott Simpson by one stroke from former champion Tom Watson.
5 Liverpool and Spurs.
6 a) LA Raiders   b) Tony Jacklin   c) Arthur Ashe.

EMLYN'S TEAM
1 Great Britain, in Paris, 1900. France took silver, Belgium bronze. Only three nations took part.
2 Gordon J. Brand (England).
3 Fatima Whitbread in the ladies javelin. She threw 76.64 metres to add the world title to her European crown, and beating world record holder Petra Felke into second place.
4 Clive Rice.
5 Flach and Seguso (USA).
6 a) Ben Nevis   b) Southampton   c) Evonne Cawley, née Goolagong.

MYSTERY PERSONALITY

BILL'S TEAM   Ed Moses, the American athlete who is the World Champion and the Olympic Champion in the 400 m hurdles.
EMLYN'S TEAM   Chris Evert, three times Ladies Singles Champion at Wimbledon and six times winner of the US Open.